CW00539136

BRASSEY'S WORLD MILITARY TECHNOLOGY

MILITARY ROTORCRAFT

BRASSEY'S WORLD MILITARY TECHNOLOGY

Series Editor: Colonel R G Lee, Royal Military College of Science, Shrivenham, UK

Incorporating Brassey's earlier Land Warfare, Air Power and Sea Power series, Brassey's World Military Technology encompasses all aspects of contemporary and future warfare. Faced with the complexity and sophistication of modern hardware, the fighting soldier needs to understand the technology to communicate his requirements to a design team. The Brassey's World Military Technology series provides concise and authoritative texts to enable the reader to understand the design implications of the technology of today and the future.

Titles currently available:

Aerospace Reconnaissance   ISBN 1 85753 138 8
GJ Oxlee
Air Defence   ISBN 0 08 034759 2
MB Elsam
Air Superiority Operations   ISBN 0 08 035819 5
JR Walker
Amphibious Operations   ISBN 0 08 034737 1
MHH Evans
Battlefield Command Systems   ISBN 1 85753 289 9
MJ Ryan
Command and Control: Support Systems in the Gulf War   ISBN 1 85753 015 2
MA Rice & AJ Sammes
Explosives, Propellants, Pyrotechnics   ISBN 1 85753 255 4
A Bailey & SG Murray
Guided Weapons   ISBN 1 85753 237 6
JF Rouse
Maritime Air Operations   ISBN 0 08 040706 4
B Laite
Military Ballistics   ISBN 1 85753 084 5
GM Moss, DW Leeming & CL Farrar
Military Rotorcraft   ISBN 1 85753 325 9
P Thicknesse, A Jones, K Knowles, M Kellett, A Mowat and M Edwards
Noise in the Military Environment   ISBN 0 08 035831 4
RF Powell & MR Forrest
Powering War   ISBN 1 85753 0489
PD Foxton
Small Arms   ISBN 1 85753 250 3
DF Allsop & MA Toomey
Strategic Offensive Air Operations   ISBN 0 08 035805 5
M Knight
Submarines   ISBN 0 08 040970 9
JB Hervey
Surveillance & Target Acquisition Systems   ISBN 1 85753 137 X
MA Richardson, IC Luckraft, RS Picton, AL Rodgers & RF Powell
The Aerospace Revolution   ISBN 1 85753 204 X
RA Mason

MILITARY ROTORCRAFT

· · · · · · · · · · · ·

P Thicknesse, A Jones, K Knowles, M Kellett, A Mowat and M Edwards

Royal Military College of Science, Shrivenham, UK

BRASSEY'S
London

Copyright © 2000 Brassey's

All Rights Reserved. No part of this publication may be
reproduced, stored in a retrieval system or transmitted in any
form or by any means; electronic, electrostatic, magnetic tape,
mechanical, photocopying, recording or otherwise, without
permission in writing from the publishers.

First English Edition 1990
Second English Edition 2000

UK editorial offices: Brassey's, 9 Blenheim Court, Brewery Road, London N7 9NT

A member of the Chrysalis Group plc

UK orders: Littlehampton Books, 10 – 14 Eldon Way, Lineside Estate, Littlehampton
BN17 7HE

'

North American orders: Brassey's, Inc., 22841 Quicksilver Drive, Dulles, VA 20166

P Thicknesse, A Jones, K Knowles, M Kellett, A Mowat and M Edwards have asserted their
moral right to be identified as the author of this work.

Library of Congress Cataloging in Publication Data
Available

British Library Cataloguing in Publication Data
A catalogue record for this book is available from the British Library

ISBN 1 85753 325 9 Hardcover

Front cover photo: WAH-64 Apache attack helicopter.
(Courtesy GKN Westland)

Typeset by SX Composing DTP, Rayleigh, Essex.
Printed in Great Britain by Redwood Books, Trowbridge.

Preface

This new volume is part of a series of books written for those who wish to improve their knowledge of military weapons and equipment. It is of equal relevance to professional servicemen and women of all armed services and those involved in the development and manufacture of modern weapon systems.

The principal authors of the book are members of the Royal Military College of Science at Shrivenham. The teaching staff is composed of a unique blend of academic and military experts who are not only leaders in the technology of their subjects, but also experienced military aviators. It is difficult to imagine any group of persons more fitted to write about the application of helicopter technology to the modern battlespace.

This book aims to give the reader both a sufficient technical background and a good understanding of the tactical roles of the modern helicopter without assuming any more technical, or operational knowledge, than would be gleaned by any person who keeps him or herself informed of current developments.

In the last decade the military helicopter has truly come of age. Armed and attack helicopters have become the tip of the spear, flying and fighting in the vanguard of every modern formation. Fitted with a wide array of sensors, they have also become the eyes and ears of the commander, providing the Headquarters, ashore and afloat, with a detailed, long range, often real time, view of the battlespace. This new found ability to see further and project fighting power at greater range allows the military commander to increase the operational tempo of the forces under command to out-manoeuvre and out-fight the enemy.

Acknowledgements

The authors greatly appreciate the help they have received from other members of the Royal Military College of Science. The authors are also most grateful to Julie Sharp and John Lestwich for their assistance with illustrations and to Mr David Gibbings of Westland Helicopters for kindly providing a number of important historical photographs.

P.J.T.
A.M.J.
K.K.
M.G.K.
A.W.M.
M.R.E.

Biographical Notes

Commander Philip Thicknesse joined the Royal Navy in 1978 as a seaman officer and graduated from Lancaster University in 1981. He transferred to the Fleet Air Arm as a pilot in 1984 and flew a variety of naval helicopters before commanding his first ship. He spent 3 years at RMCS on the military staff before returning to sea to command the Type 23 Frigate HMS Westminster.

Lieutenant Colonel Alan Jones joined the Army in 1968 and was commissioned into the Royal Signals, before joining the Army Air Corps. His career has included tours in Germany, Ireland, Cyprus, Canada and the UK. Before joining the military staff at RMCS, he was heavily involved in the UK's Attack Helicopter programme.

Dr Kevin Knowles graduated from Exeter University in 1978 and joined the Cranfield University staff at RMCS Shrivenham in 1984, following his PhD research and three years' in industry as an aerodynamicist. He has taught helicopter aerodynamics to a wide variety of courses at Shrivenham and has established an international reputation for research into V/STOL aircraft aerodynamics.

Dr Martin Kellett joined Cranfield University at RMCS in 1989 from DERA Bedford, where he was engaged in research on helicopter flight control. He completed his PhD in 1993 on the subject of control law design for combat helicopters. He currently divides his time between teaching at RMCS and running his own consultancy company.

Alan Mowat has over 30 years experience of teaching all aspects of aircraft and guided weapons propulsion. He has been on the RMCS academic staff since 1970, before which he worked in the aero-engine industry for many years and in higher education.

Dr Michael Edwards is a senior lecturer in the Department of Materials and Medical Sciences at Cranfield University. Prior to entering teaching he worked for Rolls Royce, principally on materials for hot section components such as cast air-cooled blades.

Contents

List of Illustrations

Chapter 3 – Principles of Flight

List of Tables

1.
History

The early fathers of aviation

Mankind has always been fascinated by flight, envying the birds their freedom to rise above the surface of the earth and travel great distances unimpeded by obstacles on the ground. This fascination extends beyond bird flight to the hovering flight of insects and the spiralling flight of sycamore pods. Nearly five centuries ago, Chinese children played with a simple helicopter-like toy – a stick at one end of which two feathers were attached, set at a small angle to their plane of rotation. By spinning the stick between the hands the flying toy would rise vertically into the air and fly until the spinning slowed to the point at which the feathers no longer generated lift, when the device spiralled gently back to earth. How beguiling those toys must have been and how visionaries must have dreamed of a large-scale version in which they could fly. Many centuries later the great English alchemist, Roger Bacon, in his work "The Secrets of Art and nature", wrote of an instrument "by which the wings being artificially composed may beate the ayre after the manner of a flying bird." In 1438, Leonardo da Vinci sketched an "air gyroscope" of which he wrote "I find that if this instrument with a screw be well made – that is to say, made of linen of which the pores be stopped up with starch – and be turned quickly, the said screw will make its spiral in the air and it will rise high."

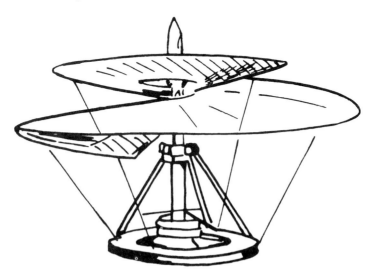

Fig 1.1 Leonardo da Vinci's Spiral

The next man to figure in the pursuit of vertical flight was a Russian Academician, Mikhail Lomonosov, the "Father of Russian Science". In 1754 he demonstrated a model helicopter before the Russian Academy of Sciences. His spring-powered design was of a coaxial type, which is to say that the two rotors were located vertically along the same axis, a design that is now the hallmark of many modern Russian helicopters.

Thirty years later two Frenchmen, Launoy and Bienvenu, constructed and flew a small spring driven machine using the same contrarotating design as Lomonosov. They were followed in England by Sir George Cayley (1773 – 1857). This remarkable polymath played an important role in many areas of engineering and science in the early part of the nineteenth century. Much of his work centred on the creation of a flyable aircraft and he very accurately described rotary flight:

"Aerial navigation by mechanical means must depend on surfaces moving with considerable velocity through the air, but these vehicles will ever be inconvenient, not to say absolutely inefficient.. for, to be of ordinary use, they must be capable of landing at any place where there is space to receive them, and of ascending again from that point. They should likewise be capable of remaining stationary, or nearly so, in the air, when required."

Known in his own day as the "Father of Aerial Navigation", he built, and possibly flew, a monoplane glider and designed a number of rotary wing machines, building the first, a twin rotored design, in 1792 and a later version of the same design in 1842. The word 'helicopter' was not coined until the mid nineteenth century when the Viscomte de Ponton d'Amecourt, combined two Greek words – 'helix', for spiral and 'pteron' for wing.

In 1842, Horatio Phillips flew the first model helicopter powered by a steam engine. This incorporated a new form of drive, the steam from the boiler passing along the rotor blades and out of jets mounted at the tips, obviating the need for an anti-torque device. Three years later Cossus, in France, had produced another steam-powered design. Perhaps the greatest breakthrough, however, was the invention, in 1876, of the internal com-bustion engine by NA Otto. By 1885 practical engines, with an acceptable power to weight ratio, were being built, making manned, powered flight achievable.

First Flights

Four years after the Wright brothers made their first historic flight, on 29 September 1907, the first manned helicopter, a Breguet- Richet Gyroplane, took off. Though it rose to the modest height of two feet it was steadied at each corner by men and could not claim, therefore, to be in free flight. That would happen two months later, again in France, with Paul Cornu at the controls of his tandem rotored helicopter, when he rose to about 6 feet and remained in the air, flying free for about 20 seconds.

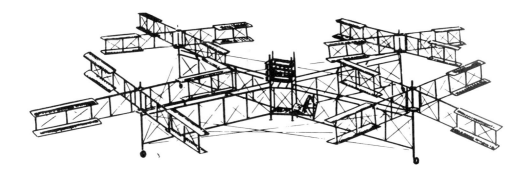

Fig 1.2 The Breguet -Richet Gyroplane No.1

Fig 1.3 Paul Cornu's Helicopter

Progress was also being made in Russia. In 1909 the young Igor Sikorsky had designed a coaxial twin bladed helicopter powered by a 25 horsepower motorcycle engine. Sadly, it proved underpowered and never flew, causing him to return to designing fixed wing aircraft. In 1912, however, another Russian, Boris Yuriev, the man who was to head the helicopter design bureau at the Soviet Central Aero-Hydrodynamic Institute (Ts AGI), built what is recognisably the first modern helicopter, incorporating a single main rotor and small anti-torque tail rotor. In one of the many delightful twists in the development of the helicopter, Yuriev later went on to supervise the design of coaxial rotored machines, following perhaps the early design of Sikorsky, while Sikorsky was to develop the main and tail rotored helicopter, the design pioneered by Yuriev.

Despite the variety of early designs, there remained a number of fundamental problems. Although engine power had become increasingly less problematic

as increasingly powerful and light engines were developed for conventional
aircraft, control stability in flight and torque cancellation proved significant
stumbling blocks to the early designers. Various methods were explored to
overcome the problems of torque: contra-rotating assemblies, anti-torque tail
rotors, tandem rotors and rotor tip drive, but each solution created some
associated complication.

Transition into forward flight and directional control of the aircraft proved
especially difficult. In 1912 a Dane called Jakob Ellehammer designed and
flew a helicopter that had a simple cyclic control system invented by GA
Crocco, an Italian, in 1906. Work continued throughout the 1920s, perhaps
best typified by the Marquis de Pescara and his No 3 design. He incorporated
a rudimentary control system into the coaxial rotored 8 bladed machine,
which allowed lift to be varied, and the rotor to be tilted to generate
directional thrust. The machine achieved a speed of 13 kilometres per hour.
Pescara was not alone. In 1924 another designer, Etienne Oehmichen, flew
the first 1 km closed circuit flight, staying in the air for 7 minutes and 40
seconds. It is an indication of the magnitude of the problems facing the
designers that it took over 16 years to achieve that small distance. To put the
flight in context, this modest aerial achievement happened five years after
Alcock and Brown flew the Atlantic.

Juan de la Cierva

The work of one man, the Spaniard Juan de la Cierva, was to solve the
control problem. Ironically, he never designed helicopters himself, but rather
autogyros, conventionally bodied and engined aircraft that used an
unpowered rotor as the lifting device instead of a fixed wing. Spurred on to
find a way of preventing conventional aircraft from stalling at low speed, he
fixed upon a rotor that was not engine driven, but freely spinning, driven by
the flow of air through the rotor and therefore unaffected by torque. His first
three designs, begun in 1920, were failures. It was apparent to Cierva that the
problem lay in the rotors, which were rigidly attached to the hub. As the
autogyros accelerated along the runway, the rotor began to generate lift, but
unequally on the advancing and retreating sides (for reasons that are
explained more fully in Chapter 3), causing the aircraft to roll over.

Cierva solved the problem by inserting a flapping hinge between the rotor
hub and each blade. The hinge allowed each blade to flap up and down, thus
altering the relative airflow over the blades and therefore the amount of lift
being generated on either side of the disc. With the modified hub added to his
new design, the C4, the first successful flight took place in 1923. Four years
later Cierva found that the blades needed to be able to move in the plane of
rotation – to lag and lead – and he added a drag hinge to his design. In
October 1925 Cierva bought one of his planes, the C.6, to England to
demonstrate to the Air Ministry and, as a result, two were ordered for trials.

Fig 1.4 The Cierva C-6 *(RAF Museum)*

In 1926 he formed the Cierva Autogyro Company. Over the next ten years over 500 of his machines were built for various customers and services. They were tried by all three services: the Royal Navy for use at sea, the Army for artillery direction and the Royal Air Force for radar calibration, for which they were used in the second world war. Cierva remained in England building his aircraft until 1936 when he was killed in an air crash at Croydon. Though a number of companies had been licensed to build Cierva autogyros, enthusiasm waned with his death. There was, however, one exception – a Scottish firm: G and J Weir, which built a series of autogyros based on the Cierva C-28. In 1937, the Company decided to concentrate on helicopter design and produced the first successful British design, the W-5, a machine which had twin rotors mounted on outriggers.

Fig 1.5 Weir W-5 *(GKN Westland Helicopters)*

In spite of Cierva's great breakthrough in articulating the rotor head, progress remained slow. In October 1930, 23 years after the first flight, a new world altitude record for a helicopter was set at 59 feet by the Italian d'Ascanio helicopter. Not until 1936, when the French Breguet-Dorand coaxial machine, fitted with a 420 hp Wright engine, reached 108 km/h, was much progress made. Within months, in Germany, the Focke-Wulf FW-61 appeared and soon began to beat all the existing records. The machine was built from parts supplied by G & J Weir and was essentially a modified version of the W-5, incorporating twin rotors mounted on lateral outriggers. Thrust was achieved using a conventionally mounted engine. In June 1937 it set new records for altitude (8,002 ft), endurance (1hr 20 mins), speed (122.55 kph), distance (80.6 km) and distance in a straight line (16.4 km). In January 1939 the helicopter flew 230km without stopping and climbed to 11,243 ft. The first practical helicopter had arrived.

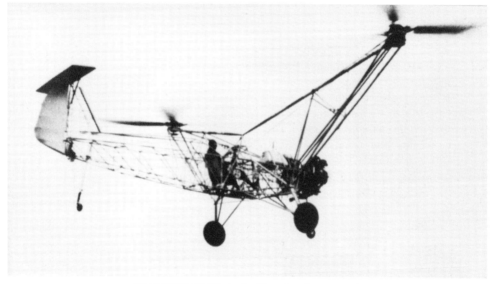

Fig 1.6 FW-61 *(DaimlerChrysler Aerospace)*

World War 2

Four countries, Japan, Russia, America and Germany built, and flew, rotary wing aircraft operationally during the war, the British helicopter programme having been shelved in July 1940. The Japanese had adapted the Kellett KD-1A autogyro as the Ka-1 and 240 were built for the Army and Navy, though little is known of how they were employed. In the Soviet Union the TsAGI A-7, again an autogyro, designed by Nikolai Kamov, was used in the reconnaissance role, armed with a 7.62mm machine gun. In the United States of America, Igor Sikorsky, who had arrived from Russia in 1919 and who had set up the Sikorsky Aero Engineering Corporation, initially to build fixed wing aircraft, patented his first helicopter design in 1931.

Fig 1.7 Sikorsky R – 4 *(P.G Harrison)*

Accepted for development in 1938, it flew for the first time in September 1939. By mid 1940, the VS-300 was able to stay airborne for up to 15 minutes. After much development, the XR-4, as it had become, was delivered to the US Army Air Corps in May 1942. In 1944, 4 R-4s were deployed to India, where one conducted a very long range rescue flight to recover four airmen whose aircraft had crashed behind Japanese lines in Burma.

In Germany, however, the helicopter was used as a weapon of war. The Fl 282 – Kolibri, designed by Anton Flettner, an aero engineer who had begun his career designing control systems for zeppelins, became the first helicopter to enter operational service, when it was accepted for the German Navy following trials embarked in a variety of warships, including the Cruiser Koln.

Fig 1.8 Fl -282 Kolibri *(DaimlerChrysler Aerospace)*

The Navy initially ordered 30 to use as anti-submarine warfare aircraft, but in 1944 1000 more were ordered for the Navy and the Luftwaffe. Work was begun at the BMW factory, but was halted by allied bombing.

Fig 1.9 Fa – 223 Drache *(Daimler Chrysler Aerospace)*

A second helicopter, the Focke-Angelis Fa 223, which looked very much like a scaled up version of the FW-61, was used by the Luftwaffe for transport, resupply and casualty evacuation. It could carry 4 men and undersling 2000 lb. of stores and was fitted with an MG15 machine gun for self-defence. It was a high performance machine, capable of climbing at up to 1,728 feet per minute, flying for just over 3 hours 40 minutes when fitted with an auxiliary fuel tank and having a service ceiling of 23,000 ft. Other helicopter designs were also developed in Germany during the war, most notably by Friedrich Dobhloff, who began development in 1942 of a series of helicopters which used tip jet propulsion.

After World War 2

With the end of the war, much of the progress achieved in Germany was transferred, by one means or another, to the United States of America. The Fa 223 Drache had been seen in the 1930s by a visiting engineer, Laurence Le Page, and during and just after the war his company, Platt le Page produced the XR-1, which has evolved over the years to become the V-22 Osprey. Anton Flettner, designer of the Fl 282 Kolibri, emigrated to the USA in 1946. He was employed by the US Navy, where it seems likely that he had contact with Charles Kaman, who took forward the Flettner rotor head in a series of designs for the US Navy and the civil market, culminating most recently in the K – Max. While these existing designs continued their evolution, one new type appeared, designed by Frank Piasecki, an engineer who had been involved with the design of the XR-1 before departing to set up his own company. Called the XHRP -1, a tandem rotored design, not unlike Paul Cornu's 1907 prototype, it entered service as the H -21 and was fondly known as the flying banana. This hugely successful design has evolved into the capable CH-47, Chinook. In France, the idea of tip jet propulsion reemerged in the Sud-Aviation Djinn, which was flown operationally in Algeria.

New wars, new roles

In Malaya (1948-60), Korea (1950-53), Indochina (1950 – 54), and Suez (1956) the helicopter increasingly proved a useful addition to the order of battle. In these early conflicts they were rarely, if ever, armed and were used mostly for recce, resupply and perhaps most memorably, from the Korean War, for casualty evacuation, saving many lives. At Suez, sixteen Whirlwinds and six Sycamores belonging to the Joint Experimental Helicopter Unit carried out the first heliborne assault into combat, ferrying 415 Royal Marines of 45 Commando and twenty three tons of their ammunition and equipment ashore in 89 minutes.

But it is in Algeria (1954 – 62) that the helicopter was first used as a weapon system. Although the French had begun the fighting along conventional lines, by the end of 1955 it had become apparent that airpower, and par-ticular, helicopter airpower, was the solution to the successful prosecution of the war. The first helicopter to be armed was the H-19 (Sikorsky S-55), which was fitted, after a variety of trials, with a 20mm cannon and two 12.7mm machine-guns, mounted in the cabin door. Far more successful, however, was the adaptation of the H-34 (Sikorsky S-58) as a gunship.

Nicknamed the Corsair by the troops, it was fitted with forward firing 20 mm cannon, 4 three tubed 73mm rockets, one 68mm rocket launcher and 4 73mm bazookas. Fitted in the windows and doors were an additional 20mm cannon, two 12.7mm machine guns and one 7.5mm machine gun. The era of the armed helicopter had arrived.

In 1958 the Alouette 2 arrived in theatre. This was the first production helicopter to be turbo shaft powered and this development would allow a great step forward to be taken. Early internal combustion engines were bulky, heavy, thirsty and were capable of only mediocre power to weight ratio. The gas turbine engine, inherently lighter, more powerful and with greater fuel economy, would allow designers and operators increased thrust and payload margins. The Alouette was fitted with either 72 x 37mm rockets or – another first – four SS10 (and later SS11) anti-tank guided missiles.

Experiments had been conducted since 1956 in the USA into arming heli-copters by the 7292 Aerial Combat Recce Company (Experimental) and in 1959 the US Marine Corps had conducted a variety of weapon trials on their helicopters, including SS11 firings. Despite the success of the French in Algeria, none of the trials resulted in any policy to arm helicopters and when US forces first arrived in Vietnam in 1961, with a mix of Bell -47s and Vertol CH-21s, they were used as unarmed troop carriers. It was not long before the

Vietcong began to exploit the vulnerability of these unarmed helicopters as they approached their landing zones. By July 1962 the Utility Tactical Transport Helicopter Company (UTTHCO) was formed. It consisted of 15 Bell UH-1A (Huey) armed with 7.62mm machine-guns and seven or eight 70mm rockets on each skid. The 1-As were joined in Vietnam by eleven Huey 1-Bs, a more powerfully engined helicopter which also carried two twin machine gun systems, hydraulically powered and aimed through a sight mounted in the cabin roof. The task of these gunships, as they came to be known, was to provide aerial firepower and protection to the unarmed troop helicopters on their approach to defended landing zones.

In 1964, as a result of experience gained with the Huey gunship, the US Army submitted a requirement for the Advanced Aerial Fire Support System (AAFSS). After competition, Lockheed was awarded a contract to develop the AH – 56A Cheyenne, a highly complex compound helicopter. Development progress was, perhaps inevitably, slow and the US Army had an increasingly urgent requirement for a new gunship. Bell, the company which had competed unsuccessfully against Lockheed with their 209, continued to develop the helicopter as a private venture. It was resubmitted to the US Army in late 1965 and in April 1966 the first 100 AH-1 Cobras were ordered. Arriving in Vietnam in September 1967, these new helicopters, armed with a variety of weapons: miniguns, cannon, grenade launchers and rockets, changed the way in which combat operations were conducted.

The Vietnam War demonstrated, beyond any doubt, the utility of the helicopter on the battlefield. Since then it has appeared in every conflict from the Falklands to Afghanistan and, most recently, the Gulf, where the new version of the attack helicopter, the AH-64 Apache, made a dramatic and extremely successful contribution to the air land battle. The helicopter has matured, arguably, into the most versatile vehicle in military service today, capable, as shall be seen in the next chapter, of a wide range of roles in every military environment. Indeed, it is this maturity and versatility that has prompted the idea of 'Air Manoeuvre' and the formation, in the United Kingdom, of the Air Manoeuvre Brigade – a formation to be equipped with attack and support helicopters capable of striking deep into enemy territory, delivering weapons and men to battle where the enemy least expect.

The helicopter at sea

The development of the helicopter at sea has followed very similar lines. The idea of operating helicopters from ships was first explored by the German navy before the second world war. The Flettner 265 was the first helicopter to be designed for anti-submarine warfare and trials were conducted on board the light cruiser Koln, which was modified with a landing platform fitted over one of the after 5.9 inch turrets.

Fig 1.10 Fl- 265 conducting deck trials *(DaimlerChrysler Aerospace)*

6 prototypes were ordered by the navy, but the helicopter was not produced because the Flettner 282, an advanced 2 seat version of the Fl 265, was chosen instead. After successful sea trials from the Koln, the helicopter was ordered into mass production for the navy. 30 prototypes were ordered, of which 22 were completed, though in 1944 an order was placed for 1,000 machines for the navy and Luftwaffe.

In America, Sikorsky was also hard at work on his helicopter design and in 1943, some years later than the Germans, his R-4 was used by the Army to conduct deck trials from a tanker and then a transport ship. A number of the helicopters were transferred to Britain and designated the Hoverfly.

In 1948, Westland Aircraft acquired the rights to build the Sikorsky S-51, a helicopter developed in the US for the army, but also used by the navy and Marine Corps. Significantly, the agreement with Westland was very favourable, allowing the British company great freedom, not only to develop and improve Sikorsky's design, but also to market the aircraft throughout the world (except in America and Canada). The Dragonfly, as the helicopter was known in Britain, first flew in 1948 and was ordered for the Royal Navy and Royal Air Force for Search and Rescue duties. In the navy they were initially used as 'plane guards', a task that required them to hover alongside the aircraft carrier during fixed wing operations, ready to pick ditched aircrew from the water. A destroyer had previously done this task and it was immediately clear that the helicopter was a far more effective and economical vehicle for the job.

Fig 1.11 Westland Whirlwind *(GKN Westland Helicopters)*

With newer and more powerful helicopters like the S-55, built under licence by Westland as the Whirlwind, both the US and Royal Navy began to explore new capabilities such as ASW and troop carrying. Throughout the 1950s a variety of helicopters were flown from aircraft carriers and other large platforms, but it was not until Westland produced the Wasp in 1958 that the possibility of operating from much smaller warships with only a single spot flight deck emerged. After extensive trials by the Navy and the Royal Aircraft Establishment at Bedford, the helicopter was ordered into production and entered service in 1963.

Fig 1.12 Westland Wasp *(GKN Westland Helicopters)*

98 Wasps were built for the Royal Navy and were operated from all the major classes of frigates and destroyers. The helicopter had an ASW capability, carrying either torpedoes or depth charges and an ASUW capability, for which it was equipped with the AS 12 missile. With the helicopter, the small warship was able to engage the enemy beyond the visual and radar horizons, allowing a single frigate to increase its area of influence by hundreds of square miles. A new age in naval warfare had arrived. The utility of the naval helicopter, its roles and weapon systems, is discussed in more detail in subsequent chapters.

2.
Roles

From the beginning the helicopter has been used in a variety of military roles. Different countries developed the helicopter in different ways. The first German helicopters, the Fl-282 Kolibri and Fa-223 Drache, both of which saw service in World War 2, were fighting machines.

The American R-4, designed and built by Igor Sikorsky, was used initially as a search and rescue vehicle, both at sea and over land. Germany was the first country to operate a helicopter from a ship, when the FL-265 was successfully trialled on board Koln in the early years of the war. They were also the first to arm a helicopter. The first gunship appeared in Algeria in the 1950s, when the French armed their H-34s with a mixture of cannon, rockets, bazooka and machine gun. The British Joint Experimental Helicopter Unit performed the first aerial assault using Whirlwinds flown from HMS Ocean and HMS Theseus at Suez in 1956 and helicopters of many types were used in Malaya in the early 1960s.

Fig 2.1 **Bristol Belvedere with loadlifting strop**. (GKN Westland Helicopters)

Without doubt, though, the Vietnam war was when the helicopter came of age. It was employed in every role and became the workhorse of the battlefield, delivering troops and supplies, providing aerial rocket artillery and fire support, ferrying casualties and enabling commanders to command from the air over the battlefield.

Limitations

Military helicopters are complex and expensive machines, highly and broadly capable and yet still limited in what they can do and in what conditions. They are traditionally seen as being vulnerable, unreliable, weather dependent and costly to maintain. At the same time, they are seen as highly versatile, are able to move rapidly around the battlespace and thus increase the tempo of operations, can carry large and varied amounts of weaponry and sensors, can use terrain to mask their presence in a way that fixed wing aircraft cannot and can operate beneath the radar horizon, flying within the nap of the earth. They can also carry and deliver large amounts of a wide range of munitions and can operate in close conjunction with ground forces in a way that fixed wing aircraft cannot.

For all this capability, helicopters still suffer from fundamental limitations. They are still slow, relative to fixed wing aviation, even though they are far quicker than the ground forces they support. In addition, all current helicopters are still heavily limited by flight in icing conditions and fog. Although many modern helicopters have reasonable anti-ice systems, including heated mats on rotor blades and engine intakes, ice can still accrete on the aircraft and cause damage.

Fog and cloud still continue to present an enormous limitation when flying close to the surface of the earth. Thermal imagers are severely degraded by fog and active radar systems, even in the millimetric waveband, cannot generate an image with sufficient resolution to pick out hazards like power lines. There are a number of novel technologies under development that are discussed in Chapter 10, but until they reach the frontline, helicopters will remain unable to fly in the nap of the earth in fog.

Finally, it has always been believed that helicopters are especially vulnerable to ground fire. The fact that, between 1966 and 1971, 4,869 helicopters were lost in Vietnam is often used as evidence to support this claim. In fact, of those figures, there were 2,587 losses to enemy fire. The remainder were classified as operational accidents. In the same period, US helicopters flew over 36 million sorties, losing a helicopter every 21, 000 sorties, with a helicopter downed every 13,461 sorties and one hit by enemy fire every 1,147 sorties. Those statistics seem actually to demonstrate how invulnerable the helicopter is on the battlefield and just what a difficult target it is to engage and destroy.

Design differences between land based and ship based helicopters

It is often assumed, wrongly, that land and sea based helicopters are identical and interchangeable. This assumption is most common in the support helicopter fraternity, who can be led to believe that it is simply a matter of flying their aircraft to a ship and operating from it. Nothing could be further from the truth. To operate a helicopter in a maritime environment requires a set of design characteristics that are not required of a land-based aircraft. Until recently, this has been of little concern to the land based helicopter community, but with the emergence of the idea of expeditionary operations and the ability to project power from the sea, independent of host nation support, it is apparent that not every helicopter is capable of prolonged ship borne operations.

Ships, even large ships like aircraft carriers, lack deck space. Aviation capable ships are always required to embark more aircraft than there are flying spots and it is therefore essential that the helicopters are foldable. With powered blade and tail fold, large support helicopters can be removed from the flight deck and stowed alongside the island or in the hangar below. Although land based helicopters like Puma and Chinook can be stowed in the hangar, they have to have their rotor blades removed. Unlike a helicopter fitted with a powered folding system that can start up, spread its blades and fly, those helicopters that have to have their blades refitted require ground and flight testing to ensure the correct rigging and tracking before they can recommence operations. This evolution can take several hours, taking up valuable deck space in the meantime. In essence, this means that non-maritime helicopters can be transported by ship, but not operated from ships. To add a powered folding system is not only financially costly, but also adds significantly to the weight of the helicopter. In the case of the EH101 Merlin, the additional weight is about 330kg, the equivalent of about 30 minutes of fuel.

Fig 2.2 Operating from a moving runway *(British Crown Copyright/MOD)*

Maritime helicopters also differ from their land-based counterparts in that they have to operate from a moving runway that is unsheltered from the wind. Maritime helicopters tend to be fitted with very powerful rotorbrakes, capable of stopping a rotor from full power in over 60 knots of wind in under 30 seconds. In contrast, the Puma has a starting and stopping limit on the rotor of only 35 knots, a severe limitation at sea. To cope with the pitch, role and heave of a deck, maritime helicopters require very sturdy, wheeled undercarriage, capable of absorbing high landing forces.

Until recently, land based aviation has taken place in an electronically clean environment, relatively unclutterd by high-powered radar and radio transmitters. At sea, the opposite is true and maritime aircraft have to be designed with a high degree of Electro Magnetic Compatibility, in order that they neither interfere with nor are interfered by ship borne high-powered transmitters.

There are many other significant differences between the two types of aircraft. Radios, navigation systems, survival systems, rescue winches and in flight refuelling equipment have all been adapted over the years to allow helicopters to operate fully from sea. Perhaps the final and most distinguishing feature is the way in which they are built. The salt laden atmosphere of the maritime environment is highly corrosive, especially to aircraft built using traditional magnesium alloys. To protect against salt corrosion, maritime helicopters tend to use aluminium alloys and composite materials. Engines have built-in fresh water compressor washing points to remove salt accretion from the compressor blades and the aircraft themselves are regularly washed and covered with light oils to keep the salt at bay.

In summary, it should be clear that there is more to operating a land-based helicopter from a ship than is immediately apparent. The problem is that a fully marinised helicopter is significantly heavier and more expensive than its more rudimentary land-based version. The choice is between fewer more capable helicopters, or a greater number of less capable ones. The temptation will always be to go for more, but the risk is that they will be unable to operate in a sea based expeditionary operation.

Command and Control

In both the land and maritime battle, military helicopters use a variety of sensors to gather information. An important consideration is the way in which the information is used by the helicopter. Different services use their helicopters in very different ways to achieve the mission. For example, while a Royal Naval Lynx might operate autonomously, searching, locating, identifying and, if necessary, engaging appropriate targets, an American naval Seahawk helicopter would be more likely to operate as an extension to the sensors of its parent ship, transmitting the data gathered back to the ship and engaging targets as instructed by the ship. Similarly, in the land battle, helicopters operate under a greater degree of positive control. Much of this difference is due to the way in which aircrew are trained , not only how to fly their machines, but how to fight.

Maritime

Anti-Submarine Warfare (ASW)

The maritime battle is different from the land and the air battle in one very specific area. Fighting takes place above and below the sea surface and each medium requires a specific set of sensors and weapons. Platforms tend to be optimised to fight in one or other medium and, until the end of the cold war, anti-submarine warfare was, for the maritime helicopter, the principal capability.

Fig 2.3 The Merlin ASW Helicopter *(GKN Westland Helicopters)*

In the anti-submarine battle, helicopters proved themselves to be the greatest threat to the submarine. Equipped with both active and passive sonars, they have the great advantages of speed and, crucially, invulnerability against counterattack by the submarine. Capable of operating at considerable range from their own ships, often up to a hundred miles from the main force, helicopters can locate, track, identify and, if necessary, attack submerged hostile submarines long before the submarine can get sufficiently close to the force to threaten it with its own weapons.

The choice of whether to use active or passive sonar depends largely on the type of submarine and its proximity to friendly shipping. Nuclear powered submarines, though fast and deep diving are, relative to diesel powered submarines, noisy. Noise radiated from gearboxes, powertrains, and the blades and shafts can all be detected passively. Helicopters and fixed wing maritime patrol aircraft operate by sowing fields of sonobuoys. The sonobuoy consists of a small floating buoy that contains a radio transmitter and a hydrophone. It is dropped from the aircraft or helicopter and, on entering the water, it releases a hydrophone, which sinks, attached by a wire, to a predetermined depth. Sounds picked up by the hydrophone are transmitted up the wire to the buoy and then on the radio uplink to the aircraft where they are processed and displayed to provide range, bearing and speed information on the target. Every submarine has a specific acoustic signature and, consequently, a high degree of identification can be achieved.

While passive sonar is highly effective against the fast nuclear submarine, it is markedly less so against the conventional submarine. Once submerged, the boat will use batteries to power silent electric engines, making itself effectively immune to passive detection. In this case active sonar is preferred. The helicopter establishes itself in the hover and lowers into the water a sonar transducer. The depth of the transducer can be varied in order to exploit the varying acoustic properties of the water column. The transducer radiates pulses of sound that reflect off objects within range. Range, bearing from the helicopter and the speed of the target and therefore be determined. Pairs or groups of dipping helicopters can track and prosecute the submarine, with one helicopter holding contact in the dip while the others jump to a new dipping position.

Torpedoes and depth charges are the weapons used to attack submarines. Depth charges are cheap and simple, being no more than a high explosive charge initiated at a given depth by a hydrostat. As such, they are of limited effectiveness. Modern torpedoes, on the other hand, are very much more effective and are really underwater guided missiles. They use high frequency, high definition sonar to detect, track and home to the target and a variety of warheads designed to penetrate the pressure hull of the submarine.

Anti-Surface Unit Warfare (ASUW)

Not every navy can afford to project power at sea from aircraft carriers alone. Helicopters flown from warships with only small flight decks can dramatically extend the reach of that ship. Until the advent of the helicopter at sea, a ship was limited by the range of the horizon and fought its engagements either visually or with radar assistance. With an embarked helicopter, capable of operating up to 100 miles from its ship, targets can be located and engaged at the limit of the helicopter's range, not just by the helicopter with its own weapons, but also from the ship. The advent of long range surface to surface missiles like Harpoon mean that the enemy can be engaged well over the horizon, with the ship's helicopter providing Over the Horizon Targeting.

Typically, modern naval helicopters are fitted with long range radar for active search and ESM and thermal imaging sights for passive search. There are a variety of anti-ship missiles currently at sea. The majority have reasonable range, allowing the helicopter to attack the target while standing off outside the engagement range of the ships own air defence systems. Though the helicopter can cover a large area of sea using its radar, it is more common for the maritime helicopter to conduct its search passively, using ESM and thermal imagers, in order to conceal its presence from the enemy, using active radar only when required for accurate positioning and for target illumination when firing a missile such as Sea Skua, which has a semi-active radar homing seeker.

Airborne Early Warning (AEW)

With one exception, maritime AEW is conducted by fixed wing aircraft. The exception is the Westland Seaking Mark 3. Although powerful shipborne radars can provide a radar picture to a range of several hundred miles, because of the curvature of the earth's surface, that radar picture will not include information on air targets flying beneath the radar horizon. AEW aircraft can be stationed at range from the force and in a position to illuminate the portion of the sky not covered by ship radars.

Fig 2.4 Westland Mk 2 AEW Seaking (GKN Westland Helicopters)

The AEW Seaking operates with a crew of 3: one pilot and two observers, both of whom are qualified Fighter Controllers. On station they can be assigned aircraft on Combat Air Patrol (CAP) that they can give either positive or advisory control in order to intercept hostile aircraft. The helicopter is equipped with an advanced version of the Searchwater radar fitted to the Nimrod Maritime Patrol Aircraft. The Observers are assisted by Link 16, IFF and GPS to enable them to play a full part in the air battle and the new command system in the aircraft will allow them to track 600 air and surface contacts.

Support

Amphibious warfare is one of the core capabilities of most large navies. The ability to project power from the sea, independent of Host Nation Support and free to pick the time and place to commit forces ashore, is key to the notion of modern expeditionary warfare. Embarked Commando forces, such as the Royal Marines and the US Marine Corps, need to be transported ashore quickly. Since the first heliborne assault at Suez, over 40 years ago, helicopters have been a key to success in amphibious operations.

Fig 2.5 Westland Seaking Mk.4 (GKN Westland Helicopters)

The actual requirement is straightforward. A helicopter capable of carrying a useful number of men, at speed, over a reasonable distance, is all that is required. The helicopter should also be capable of carrying underslung loads, as this is what it will spend the bulk of its time doing. Although conventional commando helicopters are being challenged by novel rotorcraft such as the V-22 Osprey, it is arguable that the great advantage of the Osprey, speed, is only of real significance in the initial assault, when the first wave of assault troops is being landed. Thereafter, once the beach head is secured, it is the load- lifting capability of the helicopter that is of most value and it would seem that a rotorcraft like a V-22 would be very difficult to operate underneath of during loadlifting operations, because of the very high disc loading resulting from the small rotor diameter.

Secondary Roles

In addition to the principal roles outlined above, the maritime helicopter must also be capable of performing a wide variety of secondary roles. It must be able to transfer personnel and stores, both internally and underslung, between ships underway and places ashore. It should be able to conduct search and rescue missions in most weather and sea conditions and be capable of performing a stable hover above the rescue zone, at night, in foul weather and with no natural horizon or external reference. The US Navy uses dedicated support helicopters at sea whose primary mission is the transfer of stores and personnel between ships underway.

Fig 2.6 Sea Knight helicopter *(Boeing)*

Land

Reconnaissance

The reconnaissance, or observation, role was arguably the earliest one defined for helicopters, as it was for other early forms of aviation, such as balloons and light aircraft. The ability to see further and further, with greater accuracy and understanding, remains a core military requirement. The general term "reconnaissance" embraces a number of disparate activities. First, there is the need for areas of operational significance to be searched exhaustively for enemy activity and the resulting information to be collated and passed back for intelligence analysis. Missions might include relatively straight forward patrolling tasks, or form part of a major operational screening task to ensure areas of battle-space are kept clear of hostile forces. Alternative reconnaissance tasks might include the need to carry additional passengers, taking specialist engineers to examine routes and the "going" of ground, obstacles, bridges, defences etc., or commanders to study terrain. Missions in support of other aviation operations, such as identifying attack helicopter fire positions and guiding formations will all be required. Sensors with the appropriate capability and platforms with adequate stealth, capacity and self-protection are necessary, depending on the task's specific requirements. These factors dictate a range of platform requirements. Whilst small utility helicopters are perfectly adequate for many of these tasks, once contact with the enemy is likely, then the reconnaissance helicopter becomes increasingly similar to the attack helicopter – indeed, in Chapter 7 the overlap in roles and functionality is shown to be blurred in combat. This blurring is evident at the other end of the spectrum as well. In Bosnia, the Apache attack helicopter was used with great effect to monitor troop movements and to report on them. Using its effective electro-optical sensors, it was able to detect and identify the opposing forces and to transmit live pictures, over specially installed wide band digital links, direct to those attempting to achieve disengagement of opposing factions. Moreover, it had the onboard firepower to enforce the disengagement if required to do so.

Fire Direction

The role of fire direction springs directly from the ability to conduct reconnaissance and observation. In the British Army, the role of airborne observation post (AOP) was the helicopter's primary mission. It remains an important one for any helicopter with the necessary sensors and ability to communicate with direct fire command systems. A single helicopter could, in essence, control the entire artillery of a force if required. But fire direction involves the control of any other weapon system. Typically, using lasers to direct fixed wing attacks, or to target laser seeking weapons – from any platform. Increasingly, target information will be sent automatically from one platform to another using digital burst transmissions to pass very accurate GPS based data.

However, the scope of reconnaissance capability has been greatly increased with the introduction of radar battlefield surveillance systems. The Longbow system on the Apache is esssentially a "target engagement" system, albeit providing a powerful reconnaissance and intelligence tool – particularly since so many platforms will be equipped with the radar and associated digital transmission capability. Other forces though have developed ground surveillance systems to provide ground commanders with an operational level of information support. These include the Italian "Creso" and the French "Horizon"(Helicoptre d'Observation Radar et d'Investigation sur Zone) system and are designed to complement other ground surveillance platforms, such as JSTARs and ASTOR. Creso incorporates a doppler radar antenna in a chin-mounted radome on an Agusta-Bell AB-412. It gives 360 degree coverage, with the ability to detect small moving targets out to about 100 kms – depending on the weather. This is complemented by an Electronic Support Measures (ESM) suite, based on an Italian Navy EW helicopter system, to analyse radar emissions. It also includes its own defensive EW system and the ability to transmit data to ground based control stations. Mounted on Eurocopter AS 532 UL Cougars, the French Horizon system is broadly similar. Working out to some 200 km, the radar is mounted on a arm which swivels down to be suspended under the helicopter for operation. In many ways, the mission conducted by the Horizon can be likened to that envisaged for the American JSTARS or the British ASTOR. The principal difference is that while both JSTAR and ASTOR require a runway to operate from, the Horizon helicopter can operate from anywhere, even from a ship.

Clearly, the fixed wing solution, being bigger, brings greater capability and range, but relies crucially on either Host Nation Support or in flight refuelling. The helicopter solution, though less capable, brings a capability which may be more readily deployable and more suited to the types of expeditionary operations envisaged by the west.

Battlefield Support

The role of the support, or utility, helicopter is one that is so all-pervading that it is generally taken for granted – but it's loss can diminish the tempo of operations and risk isolating deployed forces. Tasks include: large scale movement of combat supplies, including munitions and fuel; troop deployments; carriage of vehicles; movement of casualties, prisoners and stores. It can also include the movement of large items (say a radio station, or its mast) into inaccessible locations. Support helicopters range in size from the ubiquitous Bell UH-1 Iroquois (much better known as the Huey) to the large capacity Mi 26 "Halo" (which can carry up to 20,000kg). The Huey has been the mainstay of the US Army and many, many other forces since its introduction – some 40 variants (including test-beds) with at least 67 countries. The most recent variant has 4 blades and twin engines and has fulfilled many functions in land and maritime forces, as well as its prolific employment in the civil market. The newcomer is the Bell V-22 Osprey, the first operational tilt rotor aircraft, which trades payload capacity to achieve fast deployment and long range.

Specialist support helicopters might include the Sikorsky MH-60G Pave Hawk, used to support Special Operations and especially equipped with advanced navigation equipment, an all-weather radar, a retractable in-flight refuelling probe and internal auxiliary tanks and 200 foot rescue hoist.

Armed Action

Though the army attack helicopter is dealt with specifically in Chapter 9, it is worth spending a little time reviewing the evolution of this very specialised role, as armed helicopters are used by many forces worldwide. The difference is more than semantic. In essence, the Attack Helicopter is optimised for one role, while the armed helicopter has many. At present, the dedicated attack helicopter is only seen in the land battle. Maritime helicopters, especially those designed to operate from single spot ships, tend to be multi-roled and are therefore armed helicopters.

In recent years, military helicopters have become associated primarily with the more dramatic and destructive of missions. This is primarily due to such images as the Apache during the Gulf War and the Hind in Afghanistan and Chechnya.

Fig 2.7 Hind *(British Crown Copyright/MOD)*

Most helicopter platforms are capable of carrying some form of weapon system, with a number being designed specifically for armed (or attack) operations. The evolution of weapons on helicopters, the wide spread of systems utilised, the complex design implications and the range of armed, or attack, missions is dealt with in Chapter 8.

Air to Air Combat

It is hard to judge whether or not the air-to-air battle between helicopters will take place. With the growing presence of attack helicopters on the battlefield it has been argued that the most effective counter is the dedicated anti-helicopter helicopter. Operating within the same flight regime and with a similar performance envelope, it is quite possible that a helicopter is the best vehicle to counter another helicopter. Though helo versus helo engagements have been likened to two drunks fighting in a telephone box, a helicopter would seem to have a greater chance than a fixed wing aircraft of bringing down another helicopter. In 1939 the Luftwaffe conducted a trial pitting 2 fighters, an Fw 190 and a Bf 109 against a Flettner 265. Gun camera film from the fighters showed that neither aircraft was able to get into a firing position on the helicopter. It could be argued that nothing much has changed. Increasingly, attack helicopters are being armed with AA missile systems and these are discussed further in chapter 8.

Casevac

Closely aligned with the general support function is the role of casualty evacuation. Critical in saving severely injured personnel, helicopters have been widely used in every operation, saving countless lives. The early "Dustoff" Hueys in Vietnam, with only minimal specialist equipment, have been succeeded by specialist aircraft such as the US Army UH-60Q Black Hawk and the Boeing MD Explorer, 400 of which are being procured as medevac helicopters.

Fig 2.8 MD Explorer *(Boeing)*

Similar in concept to current civil medical helicopters, these will include specialist equipment, such as defribillators, ventilators, various gas and fluid dispensers and a full medical team of surgeons when needed. The aircraft comes with a full Mission Equipment Package (MEP) to enable it to operate and survive in a combat environment.

Airborne Command and Control

Helicopters can play a key role in enhancing commanders ability to maintain effective command and control over formations, or discrete operations. Gulf War commanders believed that the use of helicopters in this role gave a 40% improvement in some types of units combat effectiveness. Hitherto, the actual capability provided was little more than the ability to move commanders fast to specific areas of the battlefield and to provide them with effective communications to take control of operations from the air. The US Army Airborne Command and Control System (A2C2S) system, mounted in a Black Hawk, will be issued at a scale of 6 per Division and 12 per Corps. The cabin space of the helicopter can be fitted with up to five reconfigurable operational work stations, with large flat panel colour displays, all interactively interfaced on a wideband Ethernet to communicate with many out-stations. These could include GPS, JSTARS, satellites (and their products), UAVs, EW, special forces, reconnaissance units, ground and aviation tactical commanders, naval forces and, of course, the ground based tactical operational command posts. This would allow a commander to take to the air with considerable situational awareness.

Not to be underestimated are the important liaison tasks, carried out by light helicopters such as the Eurocopter Gazelle, or OH-58A. These are vital in taking key stores, personnel and cryptographic material rapidly around the battlefield. These light helicopters can of course be used for other roles, including both armed and reconnaissance, but they are increasingly peripheral in those functions due to small weapon load, poor survivability, low speed and range.

Electronic Warfare

Electronic Warefare (EW) is usually shrouded in secrecy. Increasingly, though, military helicopters are equipped with Electronic Support Measures (ESM) systems as part of their survivability package. These equipments allow the helicopter to play an important role in the passive EW battle. The US have recognized this in their Blackhawk "Quickfix" variant. The exact configuration is uncertain, but there seems no reason why electronic listening equipment, for both radio and radar channels, together with jamming equipment, should not be carried. Helicopters provide highly mobile passive and active EW platforms, capable of accurate position locating. Furthermore, the ability of the EW helicopter to operate at altitude allows it to locate enemy radar and comms systems at considerable range while remaining invulnerable to attack.

Search and Rescue

The use of helicopters for fire fighting and rescue is well known in civil applications. Many of these uses have been spawned by the military requirements for each. However, Combat Search and Rescue (CSAR) is now a complex operation.

Fig 2.9 Search and Rescue *(GKN Westland Helicopters)*

The days of a single utility aircraft, tasked to rescue downed aircrew, transiting with a force package may be acceptable for major warfighting operations, but events in Bosnia have highlighted the need for a more sophisticated approach. One downed US airman resulted in a major US carrier led operation featuring many fixed wing, helicopters and surveillance systems to locate, protect and subsequently rescue the individual. All this means that participating helicopters have to be equipped to be capable of working in such a complex operation. Whilst Apache helicopters have external brackets for aircrew to clip themselves to with a strop and Rooivalk has a rear "boot" for a few men to crawl into, most operations will require a carefully constructed CSAR plan, with helicopters possessing the communications, range and self-defence capability to match it.

3
Principles of Flight

This chapter aims to describe the aerodynamic principles underlying the design and operation of helicopters. In doing this it will answer questions such as: how is a helicopter controlled? How big should the rotor be? How many blades should it have? How fast should the rotor turn? Why is helicopter speed limited? What influence do altitude and climate have on performance? What functions do the various parts of the helicopter perform?

Introduction

Helicopters are a type of rotary-wing aircraft; their rotor blades are aerofoils that generate a useful force, known as lift, at right angles to their direction of travel through the air. This is the same as the mechanism of lift generation used by the wings of fixed-wing aircraft but rotary wings have the advantage that they have their own speed through the air, independent of the aircraft fuselage. Thus, a helicopter's minimum flying speed is not limited by stall of the aerofoils, as described below. Indeed, avoiding this stalling speed limitation was the motivation behind the development of early rotary-wing aircraft, as was discussed in Chapter 1.

Fig 3.1 Typical Single main rotor helicopter configuration – Mil Mi-28 (British Crown Copyright/MOD)

Helicopter rotors are driven by an engine or engines, as described in Chapter 4. For all current helicopters the rotor drive is achieved by applying a torque to a drive shaft (via a gearbox); if the helicopter is designed with one main rotor then the reaction to this applied torque will tend to rotate the fuselage in the opposite direction to the main rotor. This torque reaction is countered by applying a horizontal, sideways force to the rear of the aircraft. This is usually achieved by using a second, smaller rotor (the tail rotor) arranged vertically on the end of a relatively long tail boom (see Fig 3.1). If the heli-copter is designed with two main rotors then no tail rotor is required as the two main rotors will be arranged to counter-rotate, thus balancing each other's torque. In this case the two main rotors can be arranged in tandem, co-axially, side-by-side (see Fig 3.2) or intermeshing (an arrangement sometimes referred to as a synchropter – see Fig 3.3). Currently, however, the single main rotor / single tail rotor configuration is the most popular and appears to offer the best design compromise for most missions.

Fig 3.2 Side-by-side twin rotor system – Foche Angelis Fa-61 (DaimlerChrysler Aerospace)

Fig 3.3 Intermeshing rotor system – Flettner Fl-282 Kolibri (DaimlerChrysler Aerospace)

The helicopter is not the only type of rotary-wing aircraft. Autogyros feature an un-powered main rotor and a separate, engine-driven propeller for propulsion. The rotor is turned, like a windmill, by the air flowing through it due to the aircraft's motion. In consequence, autogyros can not hover and generally require a short landing and take-off run. They are, however, relatively stable and compact designs. The other category of rotary-wing aircraft is the compound helicopter (see Fig 3.4), which has a powered rotor together with fixed wings and/or propulsive engines (giving jet or propeller thrust). This will be discussed further in Chapter 10.

Fig 3.4 Compound helicopter – Fairey Rotodyne (GKN Westland Helicopters)

Aerodynamics and the Atmosphere

An aerofoil is defined in Jane's Aerospace Dictionary as a "solid body designed to move through gaseous medium and obtain useful force reaction other than drag". The total aerodynamic force produced by moving any body through the air is conventionally resolved into two components: lift at right angles to the direction of travel and drag opposing the direction of travel. Lift is the useful component, since it can be used to support the weight of the aircraft. Drag is the force that needs to be overcome, by the engines in the case of helicopters. These forces, to a good approximation, are proportional to air density, the plan area of the aerofoil and the speed squared (for a fixed angle of attack). Additionally, below stall, the lift will vary approximately linearly with the angle of attack.

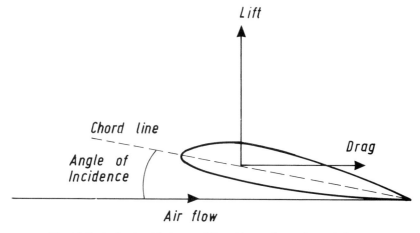

Fig 3.5 Typical rotor blade aerofoil section and aerodynamic forces

A well-designed aerofoil will generate a lift force at moderate angles of attack which is an order of magnitude (i.e. at least ten times) greater than the corresponding drag force. Such an aerofoil, designed for speeds below the speed of sound and typical of modern helicopters, has a rounded leading edge, a pointed trailing edge, is small in thickness relative to the distance from the leading edge to the trailing edge (the chord length) and has one surface slightly more curved than the other (i.e. is cambered). Note that a suitable aerofoil could be un-cambered and would still generate appropriate levels of lift provided sufficient angle of attack were used. For a typical helicopter aerofoil lift will increase, initially linearly, with increasing angle of attack; above a certain angle the lift increases at a progressively slower rate and eventually reaches a maximum. This is stall; the angle corresponding to maximum lift is the stall angle and beyond this angle (which is typically between 15° and 20°) the lift reduces and the drag rises very rapidly (see Fig 3.6).

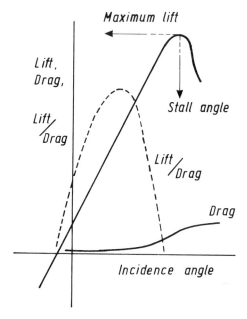

Fig 3.6 Variation of lift and drag with incidence

It was stated above that lift and drag vary with air density which consequently can be seen to be an important operating parameter, particularly when it is realised that engine power output also varies with air density. The density of air in the atmosphere is constantly changing since it depends on both air temperature and pressure. These in turn can change markedly from hour to hour and from place to place; also, both drop rapidly with increasing height above the ground. For design and performance calculations, therefore, a fixed atmosphere known as the International Standard Atmosphere (ISA) is used. The ISA is an idealised representation of the average atmospheric conditions in North America and Continental

Europe. It is based on a prescribed variation of temperature with altitude. At sea level the temperature is assumed to be 15°C and it falls, for the first 11km (36 100ft) at a constant rate of 6.5°C per km (3 280 ft). This temperature drop, and the pressure drop that accompanies it, lead to an exponential fall in air density, as indicated in Table 3.1. As described later, the power required by a rotor consists of two components, one (called the induced power) varying inversely with the square root of the air density and the other (the profile power) varying directly with the density. The first of these is the dominant component at low speeds and so the overall effect of increasing altitude is to increase the power needed by the rotor to hover. Table 3.1 shows that at 5000m altitude a typical helicopter rotor requires 20% more power than at ISA sea-level conditions. (It should be pointed out that the final column in Table 3.1 has been estimated for a helicopter of about 5300kg all up weight; for an aircraft of twice this weight the relative power figures increase only very slightly, by less than 1%.)

Although the ISA is of great value, there are clearly days and places when the sea-level air is at a higher or lower temperature. These are allowed for by adding increments or decrements to the ISA. For example, ISA + 25°C represents an atmosphere with a sea-level temperature of 40°C (15° + 25°). Since the power required to hover increases as the air density reduces and air density reduces as air temperature rises, it is the "ISA plus" atmospheric conditions which are critical for helicopter operation. These are known as "hot and high" criteria; from Table 3.1 it can be seen that to hover at 5000m on an ISA + 25°C day requires approximately 25% more power than to hover at sea level on a standard day. This is, therefore, a very significant performance criterion.

TABLE 3.1

Variation of air density and hover power with altitude – based on ISA conditions

Height above sea level (m)	Temperature (°C)	Air density (kg/m3)	Air density 1.225	Relative hover power requirement (%)
ISA				
0	15.00	1.225	1.000	100%
2500	-1.25	0.957	0.781	109%
5000	-17.5	0.736	0.601	120%
ISA + 25°C				
0	40.00	1.127	0.920	103%
2500	23.75	0.876	0.715	112%
5000	7.5	0.671	0.548	125%

Hover and Vertical Flight

In the hover a helicopter's weight is supported by the lift force generated by the rotor blades. In generating this lift force air has to be drawn down through the rotor and accelerated downwards; this induced flow through the rotor can be felt as the rotor downwash under a hovering helicopter. To accelerate air downwards requires a source of power, in this case the helicopter's engines; the amount of power required is called the induced power and is proportional to the downwash or induced velocity. In turn, the downwash velocity is proportional to the square root of an important parameter called the disc loading (the amount of thrust being generated per unit area of rotor disc) and inversely proportional to the square root of the air density. The induced power required in the hover therefore increases with increasing altitude (or atmospheric temperature); it increases with increasing aircraft weight (and consequently rotor thrust); and it reduces with increasing rotor disc area.

The rotor blades also require a source of power to rotate them against viscous drag. This power component, called profile power (because it depends on the aerofoil profile), would be needed even if no thrust were being generated. Because profile power depends on rotor aerofoil drag it is proportional to air density and, therefore, reduces with increasing altitude. The profile power also depends on the area of the rotor blades. Overall, the profile power for a typical hovering rotor accounts for less than 20% of the total power required, with the rest being due to the induced power. This percentage falls with increasing altitude and aircraft weight. Thus, the induced power is the dominant component for a hovering rotor.

The above discussion has established that the larger the rotor disc for a given aircraft weight, the smaller will be the required hover power. There is, however, a limit on the physical size of the rotor due to the flexible nature of the blades and, for single rotor aircraft, the requirement to keep the tail rotor clear of the main rotor. There is also a limit on the rotor's tip speed (typically 210 m/s), imposed by forward flight considerations. In addition, it is desirable to have the aerofoils in the hover operating well away from their stall angle. These latter two conditions combine to limit all helicopter rotors to a lifting capability of around 4.5 kN/m². Thus, the total area of rotor blade is determined by the weight of the helicopter. The rotor rotational speed is determined by its diameter (larger rotors will have to rotate more slowly) and the rotor diameter will be determined by the requirement to achieve as low a disc loading as possible. In practice the disc loading tends to have to be higher on heavier helicopters because of the constraints referred to at the beginning of this paragraph. Typical values of disc loading vary from about 175 N/m² for a small helicopter, through about 450 N/m² for a typical attack helicopter to over 700 N/m² for a heavy lift helicopter.

Rotor Control

For a helicopter to climb or descend, the lift of the rotor must be varied. There are essentially three possible approaches to achieve this: changing the speed of the rotor blades; changing the camber of the blade aerofoils or changing the angle of attack of the blades. The first of these is simple to implement (changing the fuel flow rate to the engine will directly change the rotor speed) and for this reason was used to control the rotor in one of the first successful helicopters (the Focke Achgelis Fa 61 of 1936 – see Fig 3.2). Such a system is never used on modern helicopters, for three reasons. First, the large rotor disc has a large inertia, which greatly reduces the rate at which speed and hence lift changes may be made. Thus, speed variation is a sluggish control technique. Second, the rotor is a potent source of vibration and it generates oscillatory forces at frequencies that are multiples of the rotor rotational speed. The effects of these oscillatory forces are usually reduced by careful tuning of the airframe and if the rotor speed was allowed to vary significantly this de-tuning would be impracticable. Third, autorotation (flying the aircraft without power, using its vertical motion to turn the rotor) becomes more difficult, if not impossible, if the rotor speed is allowed to fall too low.

Changing the rotor aerofoil camber can be achieved by use of a hinged flap on the trailing edge of the aerofoil, as is used to change the lift of the wings, tailplane or fin on fixed-wing aircraft. Such a scheme has occasionally been tried and at least one modern helicopter manufacturer uses a small servo flap as part of the rotor control system (see Fig 3.7). Generally, however, control flaps on helicopter rotor blades are considered too bulky and complex to provide the sole control system.

Fig 3.7 Kaman SH-2G SeaSprite with servo-flap rotor control (Kaman Aerospace)

The practical solution is to change the blade angle of attack. The angle of attack of all the rotor blades needs to be changed at the same time and whilst the rotor is rotating. This is achieved using a device known as a swash plate, or its equivalent. A swash plate consists of two parallel, circular plates, which are separated by a bearing and can therefore rotate relative to each other. The swash plate is arranged around the rotor mast, with the rotating upper plate being connected to the pitch control rods of the rotor blades (see Fig 3.8).

Fig 3.8 Westland Scout rotor head and controls (RMCS)

The vertical position of the whole swash plate assembly is adjustable, controlled by the pilot via a lever known as the collective control. Raising the collective lever acts to raise the swash plate, which therefore raises the angle of attack, or pitch, of the blades and vice versa (see Fig 3.9). The changes in blade pitch are reflected in changes in blade lift and hence in rotor thrust; they therefore enable the hovering helicopter to climb and descend vertically.

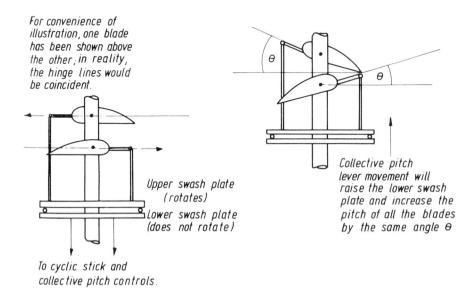

Fig 3.9 Collective pitch control

In order for the blades to change pitch, it is necessary for them to be hinged about a span-wise axis. The action of changing pitch is known as feathering and the hinge is therefore known as the feathering hinge.

When rotor lift is increased through increased collective pitch angle, the drag on the blades also increases and this tends to slow the rotor; to avoid this, more power is required from the engine. Because of this interaction between collective setting and engine power, there is often an engine throttle control on the end of the collective lever. On most modern helicopters the increased power required is supplied automatically by the engine management system. Whether it is automatic or not the increase in power required to maintain a constant rotor speed at increased collective setting will impose a greater torque reaction on the fuselage. This in turn needs to be counteracted by increased lateral thrust from the tail rotor, which can be controlled by the pilot using rudder pedals. These pedals are, in effect, a collective pitch control for the tail rotor whose blades, just like the main rotor, are fitted with feathering hinges. The rudder pedals can, therefore, be used to yaw the aircraft, i.e. rotate it to left or right about the axis of the main rotor.

Vertical Flight

A hovering rotor, as was described above, generates a downwash as an inevitable consequence of generating lift. If the rotor climbs vertically then the upward motion of the aircraft produces a flow of air downwards relative to the rotor, which helps it to generate thrust. There is, therefore, less induced power required for vertical climb than for hover. The engines, however, have to provide extra power to raise the potential energy of the aircraft and so the total power required to climb is, indeed, greater than that required to hover.

For vertical descending flight the flow through the rotor is complex. The rotor needs to generate an upward thrust to control the descent of the aircraft and, consequently needs to accelerate air downwards. The downward vertical motion of the aircraft, however, produces an up-flow of air relative to the rotor. This up-flow can interact with the rotor downwash at low vertical descent rates, sweeping some of the downwash near the rotor tip back up around the blade tips where it is re-ingested into the rotor. This establishes a so-called vortex ring state, which exists for vertical descent velocities up to about 15-30m/s (depending on the rotor disc loading). This flow pattern is very unsteady and therefore difficult to fly in; it is usually avoided by ensuring that the aircraft descends with some forward speed.

Forward Flight

Rotor Control

In order to move a helicopter in any horizontal direction, it is necessary to generate a force in that direction; for example, forward flight requires a forward thrust component. This can be achieved by tilting the main rotor. This tilt is achieved by altering the lift on each blade as it rotates; this in turn is achieved by cyclical variation of the blade pitch angle. This is called a cyclic pitch change and is commonly achieved by tilting the swash plate (or its equivalent). Swash plate tilt is controlled by the pilot via a control stick known as the cyclic stick. For cyclic pitch variation to achieve a tilt of the rotor disc each blade needs to be free to flap up and down; this is commonly achieved by fitting a flapping hinge.

Forward movement of the cyclic stick has the effect of tilting the swash plate forward, which in turn produces a cyclic change in rotor blade angle of attack (see Fig 3.10). The response to this is a cyclic flapping of the rotor blades, up over the tail boom and down over the nose. Thus, the rotor disc is tilted forwards. Similarly, if the cyclic stick is pushed sideways, the rotor will tilt that way and the helicopter will fly sideways; the same can also be said for rearward flight.

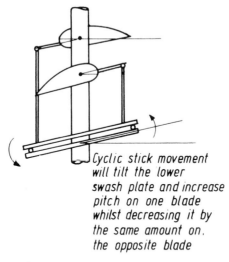

Cyclic stick movement will tilt the lower swash plate and increase pitch on one blade whilst decreasing it by the same amount on. the opposite blade

Fig 3.10 Cyclic pitch control using swash plate

By putting together the effects of collective lever, cyclic stick and rudder pedal controls, controlled flight can be achieved although various actions are needed from the pilot to maintain control during different manoeuvres. It turns out that, for almost every manoeuvre executed by the helicopter, the pilot needs to make continual corrections with all three controls. It is partly for this reason that automatic systems, designed to reduce the pilot's work load, have been introduced. These systems may be classified as Stability Augmentation Systems (SAS) or as Automatic Flight Control Systems (AFCS). They are discussed in Chapter 6.

Forward Flight Lift Asymmetry

In forward flight, the relative air speed across the blades on one side of the rotor disc is increased (the speed of the blades plus the speed of the aircraft) compared with the hover; this is called the advancing side of the rotor. On the other side, the relative air speed is reduced (the speed of the blades minus the forward speed); this is known as the retreating side of the rotor. There is also a small area of the retreating side close to the hub where the blade sees a net velocity from trailing edge to leading edge. The main effect of this so-called reverse flow region is that it contributes to vibration.

Since aerodynamic lift is proportional to air speed, a rigid rotor blade operating at constant angle of attack would generate more lift on the advancing side than on the retreating side, resulting in a moment tending to roll the aircraft. This asymmetry of lift in forward flight may be corrected in either of two ways.

i.   By varying the pitch (angle of attack) of each blade as it rotates, reducing the pitch angle on the advancing side and increasing it on the retreating side in a cyclical manner. This is cyclic pitch variation.

ii. By fitting hinges which allow the blade to flap up and down as it rotates. Because free hinges cannot transmit moments, no rolling moment can now be transmitted to the body of the helicopter. However, the resulting motion of the blades actually removes the out-of-balance moment automatically. On the advancing side, which has potentially more lift, the blade flaps up relative to its hover position. This upward motion reduces the blade angle of attack and hence its lift. The opposite effect occurs on the retreating side, with the blade flapping down and thus automatically increasing its lift. The lift force is thus automatically balanced on the two sides of the rotor disc by the flapping motion permitted by the flapping hinges.

Flapping, however, produces a problem. As a blade rotates and flaps up and down, its centre of gravity will change its distance from the axis of rotation. This causes it to attempt to speed up and slow down relative to the shaft as it rotates (so-called Coriolis accelerations). Rotor blades are not normally flexible enough in the plane of the rotor disc to allow this to happen and large forces are set up in the blades. These may be relieved by allowing the blades freedom to move in the drag direction by providing drag hinges. They allow the blades to lead or lag in their motion and are therefore also called lag hinges. They are usually fitted with dampers to damp out mechanical oscillations that may otherwise cause serious problems.

Rotor Head Design

The preceding discussion has shown that helicopter rotor blades need to be free to move about three mutually-perpendicular axes:

i.   the feathering axis to allow blade angle of attack to be changed;

ii. the flapping axis to enable the disc to be tilted and to balance out forward flight lift asymmetries;

iii. the lagging axis to relieve stresses in the blade root due to Coriolis accelerations.

A rotor having all three motions accommodated by three sets of free hinges is described as fully-articulated. The hub of the rotor, containing these hinges and their attachment to the rotor shaft is described as the rotor head, with the blades being attached to the head (see Fig 3.8). The fully articulated rotor head is the traditional helicopter design. It has a number of advantages: it offers the pilot a reasonable level of control; it is not too unstable and, therefore, difficult to fly; it is well understood and reasonably reliable. Fully-articulated rotors, however, also have a number of disadvantages:

•   because of the free hinges, they cannot transmit desirable control moments to the fuselage, so control power is limited;

•   they are mechanically complex, leading to high maintenance requirements;

•   because of their bulk, they produce high drag (up to 40% of the fuselage drag can be due to the rotor head).

Because of the disadvantages of the fully-articulated rotor head various alternatives have been introduced at different times. The two-bladed teetering rotor achieves reduced mechanical complexity by having only one flapping hinge, shared by both blades, and no lag hinges. It is more stable than a fully-articulated rotor but also less manoeuvrable and there is a limit to the amount of blade area which can be fitted before the blade chord becomes excessive.

The elastomeric bearing rotor head, although dynamically still a fully articulated design, addresses the maintenance and wear problems by replacing the free hinges in the traditional design with a single universal joint for each blade, made of layers of elastomeric (rubber-like) material reinforced by metal shims. Modern rotor head designs featuring elastomeric bearings also have multiple load paths to improve their fail-safe capabilities.

Hingeless rotor heads replace the flapping and lagging hinges with flexible elements (such as titanium forgings in the case of the Westland Lynx) but retain the feathering hinge. Such designs offer greatly improved manoeuvrability over the fully articulated head, together with lower drag and reduced maintenance requirements. The penalty, however, is a less stable aircraft which may suffer higher vibration levels. In the case of titanium, high cost is also a factor. An increasing number of helicopters are now being designed with bearingless rotors, where all three hinge movements are achieved by bending of parts of the rotor head, which is often made of composite materials.

Forward Flight Performance and Speed Limitations

It was shown earlier that a hovering rotor needs two components of power: profile power and induced power. In forward flight the levels of these depend on the flight speed: profile power increases slightly with forward speed and induced power reduces with forward speed. The reason for this latter result is that, as forward speed increases so the flow of air through the rotor increases, it therefore takes less extra effort (and less induced power) to generate the same thrust. It is a unique feature of lifting vehicles that part of the power required to propel them reduces as forward speed increases.

Increasing forward speed, however, introduces a third power component, called the parasite power. This extra component is required to overcome the drag of the fuselage (including the undercarriage, external stores, tail rotor and main rotor head). It can be shown that the drag of these parts of the aircraft increases approximately with the square of the forward speed. It follows, therefore, that the power needed to move them through the air varies with the forward speed cubed (and with the air density). Parasite power, consequently, is dominant at high forward speed but, unlike induced power, it reduces as altitude increases.

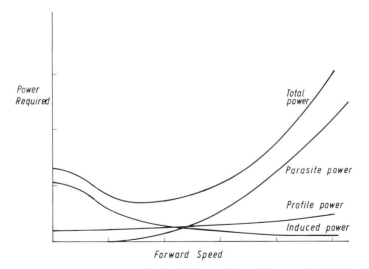

Fig 3.11 Variation of power required with forward speed for a typical helicopter

The total power required to fly a helicopter at a given speed is the sum of the three components described above. It is noteworthy that the total power required starts to fall as the helicopter gains speed (see Fig 3.11); it reaches a minimum, at a speed known as the minimum power speed, before rising increasingly rapidly. The shape of this power versus speed curve has a number of implications for helicopter operations, particularly when it is realised that the engine power output is approximately constant with speed at a value (at sea level) well above the required hover power. Eventually, the power available will cross the power-required curve and the helicopter's maximum speed will be fixed. As discussed below, however, the helicopter will be limited to a lower speed than this by the rotor aerodynamics. The minimum power speed will give the maximum endurance for the helicopter and at a slightly higher speed, known as the minimum drag speed, range will be a maximum. At the minimum power speed there is clearly a maximum of excess power available and, since this excess can be used for climbing, this speed will give the greatest rate of climb; it will also give the minimum descent rate in autorotation.

As altitude increases the power required to hover or fly at low forward speeds increases, because of the dominant influence at these speeds of induced power. At the same time, the power available from the engine reduces. Thus, an altitude will be reached at which the power available just equals the power required; this is the hover ceiling. Similarly, the power required will be increased as the weight of the aircraft is increased. Thus, there will be a maximum all up weight at which a helicopter can hover. Because of the shape of the power versus speed curve, however, it will be possible to fly at weights above the maximum allowable hovering weight, or at altitudes above the hover ceiling, by flying closer to the minimum power speed. Thus, a high weight or high altitude (or high temperature) take-off will consist of a rolling take-off in which the helicopter gains speed on, or just above, the ground; as it does so the power required is reduced and it is then able to get airborne. This operation is aided by ground effect, which is a beneficial effect of ground proximity, causing a reduced rotor downwash and consequently reduced induced power. Under extreme conditions, at the limits of the helicopter's capabilities even in ground effect, a take off may just be possible by flying in a suitable circle, since this reduces the thrust required of the tail rotor and hence its power requirement, leaving more power available to the main rotor.

The maximum flight speed of a helicopter is fundamentally limited by the rotor. As described above, forward flight brings with it an asymmetry in velocity across the rotor. To counteract the consequent lift asymmetry the retreating blade needs to achieve higher and higher angles of attack as the forward speed increases. Eventually the retreating blade will stall near the tip. This stall could be delayed to higher flight speeds by increasing the speed of rotation of the rotor. This is not a viable solution, however, because the advancing side of the rotor sees the sum of forward speed and tip speed. The tip of the advancing blade is typically flying close to the speed of sound; increasing the rotor speed will produce even higher speeds on the advancing side which will cause, among other things, a very large drag increase and a loss of lift. The net result of this is that there is an almost universal optimum tip speed for all helicopter rotors (around 210 m/s).

Other Design Features

Empennage

In the Introduction section of this chapter the need for a tail rotor was described, on helicopters with single main rotors. On most modern single-main-rotor helicopters, however, the tail boom supports not only the tail rotor but also a vertical fin and a horizontal tailplane, known collectively as the empennage (see Fig 3.12).

Fig 3.12 Boeing AH-64 Apache showing empennage (McDonnell Douglas Helicopter Systems)

The horizontal tailplane, which is invariably of aerofoil cross-section and usually cambered, will generate a down-force as the helicopter flies forward at a nose-down attitude (the natural attitude for a helicopter in forward, powered flight – see Fig 3.13) and this acts to "trim" the aircraft to a better, less nose-down attitude. Additionally, a horizontal tailplane will provide a measure of pitch stability (tending to return the helicopter to its original attitude if it is disturbed in pitch) counteracting the tendency of the main rotor to be unstable in pitch. Problems can occur if the tailplane is mounted low down on the end of the tail boom, as the main rotor wake will impinge on it at certain flight speeds, causing an un-commanded pitching which the pilot has to counteract. In some cases (Apache – Fig 3.12, Blackhawk) designers have had to avoid this problem by designing an all-moving tailplane, which automatically adjusts to the local airflow direction.

Fig 3.13 Characteristic attitude of helicopter in forward flight – Mil Mi-28s (British Crown Copyright/MOD)

The vertical fin is often needed to support the tail rotor and will be of aerofoil cross-section to reduce its parasite drag. In the event of a loss-of-tail rotor accident, such a fin can generate an aerodynamic side force (a sideways lift) provided that the helicopter has sufficient forward speed and a suitable yaw attitude. If the fin is suitably cambered then no yaw attitude will be required for the helicopter to fly stably without a tail rotor. The speed at which the fin can replace the tail rotor will be lower the larger the fin is; an excessively large fin, however, will interfere aerodynamically with the tail rotor reducing its effectiveness and provide a large drag when the aircraft is being manoeuvred in yaw. Fin design is, therefore, a compromise between survivability and manoeuvrability.

The traditional open tail rotor has a number of disadvantages.

•   It suffers from high drag in forward flight.

- It is very noisy.

- It is hazardous to personnel on the ground.

- It can be easily damaged when manoeuvring close to the ground.

- It requires long drive shafts and additional gearboxes; these drive shafts are susceptible to damage from blast waves and so can be destroyed without being directly hit.

To address some of these problems, alternative designs have been introduced over the years. Aerospatiale introduced a shrouded tail rotor, which they called a fenestron, on aircraft such as the Gazelle and Panther. Because the rotor is shrouded it has to be relatively small and this gives it a high disc loading and therefore a relatively high power requirement. To offset this inherently low efficiency, the fin is highly cambered and off-loads the tail rotor entirely at modest forward speeds. To improve the tail rotor efficiency at low speeds, when the fin is ineffective, the duct around the rotor is shaped to generate some useful thrust from the air-flow through it. Overall, the fenestron is much safer than an open rotor and it is more efficient at high speeds but less efficient at low speeds. It is quieter in the plane of the rotor but noisier to the sides. The fenestron can suffer from a serious stall problem during high speed manoeuvring because of the aerodynamic interaction between the rotor flow and the low pressure on the suction side of the fin. The main limitation to the use of the fenestron and similar shrouded tail rotors, however, is the weight of the rotor duct and tail fin which restricts such installations to small and medium sized helicopters (see discussion below on centre of gravity limits).

An alternative to a tail rotor, whether open or shrouded, for torque reaction is to use jet thrust. Such a system was used by Cierva on their W.9 of 1947, which used the exhaust from a piston engine mixed with atmospheric air to produce a horizontal air jet at the end of the tail boom. More recently Hughes aircraft, later McDonnell Douglas Helicopters now part of Boeing, developed a system called NOTAR. This combines an adjustable jet thruster with a concept known as circulation control on the tail boom. A fan at the base of the tail boom provides the air for both these systems. It is worth noting that, during the LHX design competition in the USA the requirement for reduced vulnerability of the anti-torque system was so stringent that neither of the competing designs had an open tail rotor; one used NOTAR and the successful Comanche used a development of the fenestron system.

Centre of Gravity Limitations

The centre of gravity of a helicopter (the point through which the weight acts) has to be arranged to be close to the line of the rotor mast on single rotor helicopters. This is because the aircraft hangs from the rotor, to which it is connected by hinges (the blade flapping hinges). If the centre of gravity is to the rear of the rotor mast, then the helicopter will hover tail down; to prevent the aircraft from flying backwards the pilot must apply forward cyclic. Thus, with the centre of gravity to the rear, just to hover requires some forward flight control, which in turn reduces the maximum forward thrust that can be achieved. Conversely, with a forward centre of gravity, aft cyclic control is needed to maintain trim in the hover.

To avoid limiting the flight envelope, therefore, designers and operators need to ensure that the c of g remains as close to the rotor mast as possible. The designers will ensure that items such as fuel tanks, weapons pylons and underslung load hooks are all close to the mast to avoid trim changes as the aircraft weight varies during a mission. In some cases, the hover trim is helped by providing some vertical thrust from the tail rotor by canting it at a slight angle to the vertical (Blackhawk, CH-53). If operators fit items such as armoured seats then the aircraft may have to be re-trimmed with a counter-balance weight in the tail cone. It can also be seen from this discussion that excessively heavy empennage designs can not be accommodated. The tail rotor will tend to be disproportionately bigger on larger aircraft in any case, because of the way main rotor torque varies with thrust, and so shrouded rotors become less viable above a certain size of helicopter.

Multi-rotor Helicopters

As described earlier, multi-rotor helicopters can have their rotors arranged side-by-side, in tandem, co-axially or intermeshing. With tandem configurations (see Fig 3.14) the centre of gravity position is not limited as in the above description but even here excessively rearward c of g positions cannot be tolerated because of direction stability considerations.

The common feature of all multi-rotor designs is the absence of a tail rotor. Whilst this removes the vulnerability problems discussed above it also removes the powerful yaw control which a tail rotor provides. The pilot of a multi-rotor aircraft is still provided with rudder pedals but these operate on the main rotors. With tandem and side-by-side configurations the rudder pedals apply a differential cyclic pitch control to the two main rotors, tilting them in opposite directions (left and right or fore and aft, respectively). With co-axial rotors the rudder pedals create a differential torque on the two main rotors. This is achieved simply by increasing the collective pitch on one rotor and reducing it on the other. The total thrust remains constant but the drag, and therefore torque, will increase on one rotor causing the fuselage to yaw in the opposite direction. This co-axial yaw control can be very powerful but it does depend on the main rotor power and thrust levels; yaw rates depend, therefore, on forward speed and aircraft weight.

Fig 3.14 Tandem rotor configuration – Boeing MH-47E, Special Forces variant of the Chinook
(Boeing)

Two key advantages of multi-rotor helicopters are their compact layout and the ability to fit a relatively large blade area without the bulk and complexity of a large, multi-bladed hub. This has left such helicopters to occupy a few niche roles. The tandem-rotor CH-47 Chinook (Fig 3.14) has proved to be a very successful, compact heavy-lift helicopter. The co-axial configuration has long been used in the Former Soviet Union by the Kamov design bureau for shipboard use and has been developed recently into the Ka-50 attack helicopter, which is relatively fast thanks to its large blade area.

Fig 3.15 Kaman K-Max Intermeshing rotor configuration (Kaman Aerospace)

The intermeshing rotor has been used by Kaman aircraft in the USA for compact shipboard aircraft and, more recently, in the K-MAX "aerial truck" (Fig 3.15) which is aimed at extensive underslung load roles. The side-by-side rotor configuration is used in the V-22 Osprey tilt-rotor (Fig 3.16), which is a special configuration that will be discussed in Chapter 10.

Fig 3.16 Bell-Boeing V-22 Osprey(Boeing)

Currently, the vast majority of helicopter types in service are of the single main rotor configuration. This chapter has attempted to explain the fundamentals of aerodynamics as they apply to all helicopters, with particular emphasis on single-rotor applications. This is, however, a complex field and one in which design decisions are often based on analysis of performance characteristics that are beyond the scope of this text.

4.
Engines and Transmissions

The value of the military helicopter today is due primarily to its ability to carry a useful payload over a long range or with a good endurance. For a given design, this ability depends on the engine/s and transmission, which should have a good power-to-weight ratio, coupled with low fuel consumption and a high reliability. Except for very small helicopters, which are no longer widely used by military forces, the gas turbine engine is used exclusively, in single or multiple installations.

The Gas Turbine Engine

The earliest helicopters were fitted with piston, spark-ignition (i.e. gasoline) engines because they were highly developed and offered a fair power-to-weight ratio, a good fuel consumption, good reliability and were readily available in various sizes. As the need for increased power became evident, piston engines became increasingly complex, multi-cylinder designs, their weight tended to increase and their reliability declined. Meanwhile, early gas turbines were becoming more efficient (but not yet as efficient as the best piston engines), more reliable, and, most importantly of all, were able to provide better power-to weight and power-to-volume ratios. This was particularly so of the so-called free power turbine type which dispensed with the need for a clutch in the drive train, a drawback in all piston engine installations. The gas turbine thus became the most important engine employed in helicopter propulsion.

Engine Configurations

The gas turbine engine is also widely used to propel fixed-wing aircraft. In these applications it is usually a turbojet or a turbofan, which generates a high-speed jet in developing the force to propel the aircraft forward at high subsonic or supersonic speed. In helicopters, however, the gas turbine is not used as a means of producing a force but is used to produce mechanical power in the form of a rotating output shaft which is connected to the helicopter rotor (or rotors) through a mechanical transmission system. In this form it is known as a turboshaft engine. It is a close relation of the fourth and final variant, the turboprop, widely used in modern propeller-driven, fixed-wing aircraft.

Principles of Operation

The principal function of any aero-engine, broadly speaking, is to convert

49

heat, generated by the combustion of fuel in air, into a useful form of
mechanical power. No engine is capable of carrying out this conversion with
an efficiency of 100%. Engines can be built, however, to perform at what is
regarded as good efficiency. The turboshaft is such an engine.

It is based on a sequence of continuous operations in which different
processes are successively carried out on the working medium, air, to
produce useful power. The major components which constitute the heart of
the engine, the gas generator, are shown diagrammatically in Figure 4.1 in
their relative working positions. What happens to the flow of "gas", the
combustion products, determines whether the engine is a turboshaft or a
turbojet.

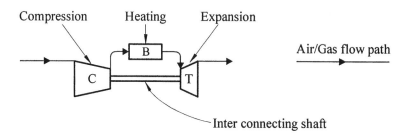

Fig 4.1 Diagrammatic layout of a gas generator

Operation

In operation, the turbine (T) receives high-pressure, hot gas (a mixture of air
and combustion products) which flows through the blades at high speed,
causing the turbine wheel to rotate. In so doing the energy content of the gas
is depleted to some extent. The mechanical energy extracted by the turbine
wheel is transmitted through a rotating central shaft to the aerodynamic
compressor (C) upstream, which behaves in roughly the opposite manner to
that of the turbine, absorbing its output. The compressor thus draws in
atmospheric air, compresses it and directs it to the combustor (B). Here the
air is mixed with kerosene and burned to an appropriate temperature before
it is directed to the turbine. The turbine then allows the hot, high-pressure
gas to flow through its blades, producing the mechanical power to drive the
compressor. These three components – the compressor, the combustor and
the turbine – form the gas generator.

In the case of the turbojet, the gas leaving the gas generator flows directly to
the nozzle (N), as shown in Figure 4.2. This type of gas turbine produces a
high-velocity jet of gas from the nozzle. The useful output of this type is the
forward FORCE on the whole engine resulting from the rearwards
acceleration of the air/gas flow through the engine. (Turbojets have been
used on compound helicopters to produce higher forward speed.)

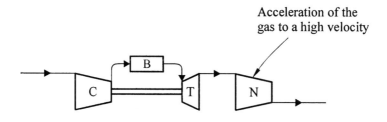

Fig 4.2 Diagrammatic layout of a turbojet engine

The turboshaft engine, in which we are much more interested for helicopter application, is shown diagrammatically in Figure 4.3. In this arrangement the gas generator, C+B+T1, behaves just as before, but immediately downstream of turbine T1 is another turbine T2. Turbines T1 and T2 are known respectively as the high- and the low-pressure turbines. Turbine T2, nearly always mechanically separate from the gas generator section, as illustrated, and able, therefore, to rotate at a different speed, is now also able to provide a drive to the rotor, the gas flowing through turbine T2 giving up much of its remaining high-temperature energy to turbine T2 and hence to the load. In the case of a helicopter, the rotor system is the load, being driven through a speed-reducing transmission. This is a typical turboshaft layout.

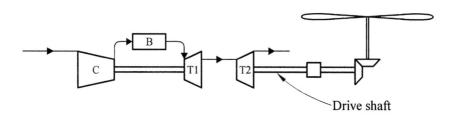

Fig 4.3 Diagrammatic layout of a typical turboshaft engine

For completeness, variations on the two schemes described above are illustrated in the simplified cross-sectional diagrams in Figures 4.4 and 4.5. The turbofan is a "bypass" variant of the turbojet and the turboprop is a fixed-wing aircraft, shaft power unit having many similarities to the turboshaft engine. This is a more important point than it might at first seem. Engine designers for many years have recognised the importance of the gas generator, or core, being adaptable to turboshaft, turboprop, turbojet or turbofan configuration.

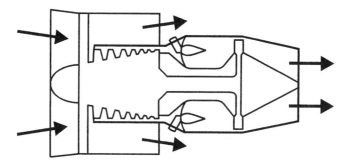

Fig 4.4 Cross-section of a turbofan engine

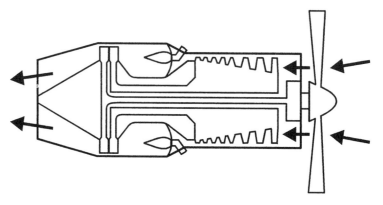

Fig 4.5 Cross-section of a turboprop engine

Types of Turboshaft

There are two turboshaft configurations which are available. They are known as the free (or power) turbine and the fixed (or single-shaft) turbine. There are several important distinctions between the two, both in their layout and application in helicopters.

The Fixed Turbine or Single-shaft Turbine

A diagrammatic arrangement of a single-shaft engine is shown in Figure 4.6 and a cross-sectional diagram of an actual single-shaft engine in Figure 4.7.

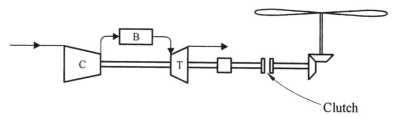

Fig 4.6 Diagrammatic layout of a fixed-turbine engine

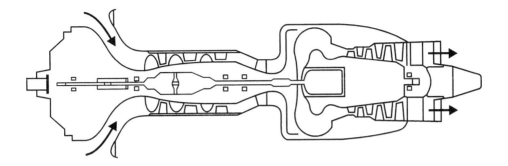

Fig 4.7 Cross-section of a turbomeca *Astazou* engine

The most important feature of this type of engine is that the output shaft, which delivers power to the gearbox and then to the transmission through a clutch, is directly connected to the to the single turbine. Thus there is a fixed relationship between the rotor rotational speed and the engine rotational speed. Since a helicopter rotor runs at approximately constant rotational speed during flight, the consequence is that the fixed turbine engine is constrained to operate at approximately constant rotational speed also. While this arrangement offered one or two advantages some years ago, before the development of Full Authority Digital Engine Control (FADEC) (see later), such as a very rapid response to a load change imposed by a sudden increase in rotor collective pitch, it also results in a rather inflexible engine. For example, since it is essentially a constant rotational speed engine, it has to be rated at a rather modest power because of the need to sustain the chosen rotational speed. There is thus a built-in power limitation which prevents the achievement of high emergency powers even for short durations. In addition, the torque–speed characteristics of the engine are not well matched to the rotor, however this shortcoming can be dealt with by the provision of a suitable engine control system. There is also a weight penalty associated with the clutch and, finally, the fuel consumption at low or moderate powers is poor compared with that at the maximum continuous power condition.

The main proponents of the single shaft type, Turbomeca in France, have built a series of such engines over a long period. Their particular design shown in Figure 4.7, the Astazou engine (installed in the Gazelle helicopter), features the output shaft emerging from the compressor, or intake, end of the engine. This contrasts with the simpler design in Figure 4.6. Apart from the mechanical design arrangements, this particular layout is no different in principle from that shown in Figure 4.6.

The Free Turbine

The free turbine engine is by far the most commonly used configuration in both single-engine and multi-engine helicopters. The main reasons for the widespread adoption of this type are its favourable torque-rotational speed characteristic (promoting rotor speed stability), reasonable fuel consumption at part-power operation and the simpler layout resulting from the absence of a clutch in the output drive train. A diagrammatic layout of a free turbine engine is shown in Figure 4.3 above.

The diagrammatic layout highlights the characteristic feature of the free turbine type, which is the absence of a mechanical connection between the gas generator (C+B+T1) and the output (power) turbine (T2), which is thus "free". In fact in a helicopter application the power turbine rotates at substantially constant speed under all conditions apart from transient states such as start-up and run-down. It is the gas generator which is free to operate over a range of rotational speeds, to enable its gas flow to be best matched to the requirements of the power turbine. It should be noted that the power required by the rotor may vary greatly according to the operating flight conditions despite the fact that the rotor rotational speed is nominally constant. Thus the freedom offered by the ability of the gas generator section to run over a range of rotational speeds is considerable. However, the "free" turbine description means no more than that the power turbine has a gas flow link rather than a mechanical link to the gas generator.

In-service Engines

An early gas-turbine engine, still very much in service in the Westland Sea King helicopter, for example, is the Rolls-Royce Gnome. This engine has a 10-stage, 8:1 pressure ratio axial-flow compressor (i.e. 10 rows of rotating compressor blades through which the air passes axially and which collectively raise the pressure 8-fold from the inlet value) which is driven by a 2-stage axial-flow turbine. The combustor in this case is a straight-through type. (Note that, in common with other engines, more stages are needed for the axial compressor than for the turbine. This is because pressure is rising throughout the compressor and boundary layer separation on the blades – stall – has to be avoided.) This gas generator supplies a single-stage free power turbine whose output shaft delivers the power at the hot (ie exhaust) end of the engine. Engines of this configuration typically incorporate "variable geometry" in several sets of compressor guide vanes (ie stator blades) and blow-off valves to ensure satisfactory handling of the engine throughout its operating envelope. Control of such early engines is normally hydro-mechanical, using a power turbine speed governor.

A later engine (1968), incorporating many novel features, is the Rolls-Royce Gem (Figure 4.9), typically rated now at around 1000hp (750kW) and employed principally in the Westland Lynx helicopter. In response to the UK MOD's requirements for low fuel consumption, high power-to-weight ratio and excellent handling characteristics, a 2-spool gas generator is used. This feature, particularly for a small engine, involves considerable added complexity, not least a total of three co-axial shafts, since the power turbine shaft delivers the output at the intake end of the engine to an integral gearbox. The low-pressure 4-stage axial-flow compressor plus the single-stage centrifugal compressor (each running at its optimal rotational speed) together provide a pressure ratio of 14:1 in the Gem 60 (compare with that of the Gnome). Note that centrifugal compressors can achieve higher pressure ratios in fewer stages than an equivalent axial flow design but at the expense of a larger diameter. The reverse-flow combustor is well matched to the radial outflow from the centrifugal compressor and also enables the whole engine to be shortened, a useful design feature. Each of the compressors is driven by its own single-stage turbine, the gas passing to the 2-stage free power turbine. The use of the 2-spool gas generator configuration obviates the need for variable geometry or bleed valves in the compressor. The high pressure ratio together with a high maximum gas temperature satisfies the need for low specific fuel consumption and high specific power. (NB Specific fuel consumption is the rate of fuel consumption compared with the power output, often expressed in kg/(h kW); specific power is the power output compared with the air flow rate , typically in kW/(kg/s), and is a measure of engine size.) In addition the Gem was the first engine to feature modular construction, a technique of design and manufacture enabling quicker and easier servicing by the replacement of large engine sections, e.g. the low-pressure compressor module or the power turbine module. Most marks of the Gem employ conventional hydromechanical control.

Since the mid-1980s Rolls-Royce of the UK and Turbomeca of France have collaborated in the design and development of a third generation engine in the 2000–3000hp (1500–2200kW) class, the RTM-322. It is sized to power single-engine helicopters in the 4000–6000kg class, twins in the 6000–12000kg class and 3-engine helicopters in the 12000–16000kg class. First run in 1985, this turboshaft was initially rated at 2100hp (about 1600kW) and is a direct competitor with the well established and widely used General Electric T700. It is the chosen powerplant for the twin-engined Westland WAH-64 Longbow Apache and the three-engined EH Industries EH-101 helicopters. The engine offers significant growth potential and easy maintainability, and is of robust construction.

Consisting of 6 modules, the engine has a single-spool gas generator (i.e. core) comprising a 3-stage axial-flow compressor (with two sets of variable guide vanes) plus a single-stage centrifugal compressor giving an overall pressure ratio of 15:1, delivering the air to an annular reverse-flow combustor. A 2-stage axial-flow turbine drives the combined axial/centrifugal compressor via a hollow shaft. The two-stage power turbine delivers its output to the intake end of the engine via a shaft running through the hollow gas generator shaft. The compressor is made of titanium, with each bladed disc (or "blisk") in the axial-flow section being of single-piece construction.

The gas generator 2-stage turbine features air-cooled first- and second-stage stator blades and first-stage rotor blades which are made of directionally solidified nickel alloy (the reasons for the use of different materials and manufacturing techniques will be discussed more fully in Chapter 5). The second-stage rotor blades are single crystal and uncooled. The power turbine blades are uncooled and made of nickel alloy. The use of turbine blade cooling and modern blade manufacturing techniques allows higher gas temperatures which, together with high pressure ratio, promote reduced fuel consumption and increased power-to weight ratio compared with previous generation engines. The RTM-322 also incorporates an inlet particle separator (which may be removed), a vital component on a present-day military helicopter installation which may have to tolerate very adverse operating conditions giving rise to intake air contaminated with sand, dirt, water, etc. Control of the engine is by a FADEC system (see later).

In the 1200–1500hp (900–1200kW) class, the tri-national MTR-390 is the outcome of a collaborative programme involving MTU of Germany, Turbomeca of France and Rolls-Royce of the UK. First run in 1989, the engine is initially rated at around 1300hp (1000kW) for installation in the twin-engined Eurocopter Tiger attack helicopter. Consisting of three modules, the engine has a 2-stage centrifugal compressor, giving an overall pressure ratio of 14:1, delivering to an annular reverse-flow combustor. The compressor is driven by a single-stage axial-flow turbine. The 2-stage axial-flow free power turbine delivers the output power to the integral reduction (and accessory) gearbox, positioned at the front of the engine, via a shaft running through the hollow gas generator shaft. The unusual twin centrifugal compressor design is adopted for a number of reasons. Combined with the reverse-flow combustor, the design results in a short, compact engine layout. The centrifugal compressor is traditionally more robust than the axial-flow design (especially in small engines) and is thus more tolerant of foreign object damage (FOD). Associated with this feature, there is no need for a particle separator in the side-facing intake. It is expected that this novel layout will give excellent reliability. The single-stage axial-flow turbine driving the compressor has air-cooled directionally-solidified nozzle (stator) blades and single-crystal rotor blades, both of nickel alloy. The 2-stage free power turbine is uncooled, with single-crystal blades. Another interesting feature is that the power turbine contra-rotates relative to the gas generator. This is said to help to raise the engine's efficiency. Finally, the engine incorporates a FADEC system.

The Transmission

The primary function of the transmission system is to transmit the power provided by the engine/s to the rotors. In a single-main-rotor helicopter this includes providing the power to the anti-torque tail rotor.

It was noted earlier that some helicopter engines have an integral reduction gearbox. This means that fewer stages of rotational speed reduction may be required in the main transmission gearbox. In all cases input speed to the transmission is much greater than the main rotor (or rotors) requires and so additional speed reduction must be provided. Furthermore, since most engines are positioned longitudinally in the fuselage but at right angles to the rotor mast, and probably displaced laterally also, the transmission must turn the drive through these right angles. This dual function may be accomplished with one or two stages of spiral-bevel gears plus two or three stages of some combination of bevel, spur/helical and planetary gears.

Twin-engined helicopters need a transmission which will accept two input drives to provide a single main output drive. This is a complex arrangement in which the power outputs of the two engines must be carefully matched. Such an installation is that in the Puma helicopter, for example. The two Turbomeca Turmo engines provide the input at 23 000 rev/min, the single output to the rotor being reduced to 265 rev/min. This is an overall reduction ratio of about 100:1 and is not easily accomplished.

Similarly, the Boeing AH-64 Apache helicopter transmission has two input shafts from the two engines' nose gearboxes (first speed reduction) driving through three additional stages of speed reduction culminating in an overall speed reduction from 20 000 rev/min at the power turbine shafts to 289 rev/min at the main rotor shaft. The tail rotor speed reduction ratio is significantly less, being approximately 4:1 (compared with the main rotor – Figure 4.8).

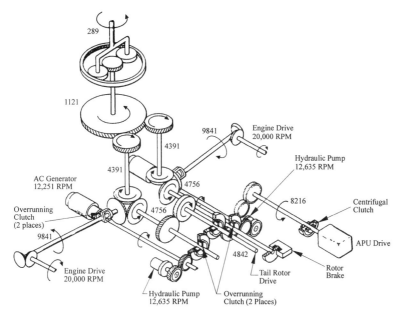

Fig 4.8 The AH-64 Transmission

It is interesting to note in passing that the Bell-Boeing V-22 tilt rotor aircraft (see Chapter 10) has a complex cross-shafting arrangement in its transmission to ensure drive to both rotors in the event of one engine becoming inoperative.

Quite apart from providing the proper speed reduction, the main gearbox and ancillaries (such as generators, pumps, over-running clutches, etc) should ideally be as light as possible, transmitting little vibration to the fuselage and offering reliable performance with a respectable overhaul time. Transmissions today are highly developed, much progress having been made in second- and third-generation helicopters. This has been achieved by raising allowable stress levels in gears through better design and the use of better materials and manufacturing techniques (see Chapter 5).

Full Authority Digital Engine Control (FADEC)

A FADEC system incorporates a computer which receives signals from many sensors (of gas temperature, shaft rotational speed, torque, etc), analyses these inputs according to the requirements designed into the software and adjusts the fuel flow to provide the required power output. The benefits of FADEC over the traditional hydromechanical control are enormous. The latter is a relatively simple system conceptually (though in practice the plumbing is complex), in which the aim is to keep the power turbine rotating at a chosen speed, irrespective of the load imposed by the rotor, by adjusting the fuel flow and hence the gas generator rotational speed and hence the gas flow to the power turbine. In addition there may be built-in over-speeding limits for the gas generator and power turbine. Twin-engine installations usually provide automatic torque matching, i.e. equalisation of the inputs to the combining/reduction gearbox.

FADEC, on the other hand, offers in addition the opportunity to run engines close to their operating limits, particularly during transient and emergency conditions, giving good handling characteristics. Automatic start sequencing, acceleration control, maximum turbine entry temperature control, positioning of variable inlet guide vanes and bleed valve, surge (i.e. compressor blade stall) and flame-out protection and power limitation are provided. Pilot work-load is reduced, enhancing mission performance. It is possible, furthermore, to incorporate built-in test features, recording "exceedances" of limits, counting engine cycles and so on, i.e. "supervisory and health-monitoring tasks".

Engine Health Monitoring

Main in-flight indicators typically available in the cockpit are power turbine rotational speed, torque and gas entry temperature and gas generator rotational speed. Complementing these on the ground there would be available for use vibration monitors, borescope inspection and magnetic detector plug inspection which together with data recorded by the FADEC system offer ample scope for condition monitoring.

IR Suppression

It is essential, for reasons that will be discussed in Chapter 7, that military helicopters minimise the infra-red signature of the engine. The aim is to reduce the temperature of both the exhaust gas and the visible hot metal parts so that the infra-red radiant energy is not detectable by sensors on the most up-to-date missiles. The approach to minimising the emissions is two-fold: cooling of the hot exhaust gas by mixing it with secondary atmospheric air drawn into a lightweight box surrounding the "buried" engine and shielding of the hot metal parts by the cool box structure. The emissions from the metal parts tend to be the dominant portion and so designs of suppressor which envelop the engine, albeit incurring some degradation of engine performance, are favoured.

Future Technology

It is clear that all aspects of performance of engines and transmissions will continue to improve so long as there is a demanding user who has to pay the acquisition and operating costs. The gas turbine engine will certainly hold its dominant position over the next generation of helicopter powerplants. There will be a significant reduction in specific fuel consumption and a significant increase in specific power through the use of improved materials, higher gas temperatures and improved turbine blade cooling techniques, improved aerodynamic design and computer-aided manufacture. A reduction in unit cost can also be expected to accompany the performance gains. Thanks to advances in methods and equipment for monitoring the condition of engines one can expect to see a steady improvement in reliability not-withstanding the more extreme regime of thermal and dynamic loading corresponding to the higher intrinsic performance.

As yet there is no indication that any manufacturer is giving serious consideration to developing a gas turbine engine with a recuperative cycle (as used in the Abrams main battle tank). The improvement in specific fuel consumption at both full power and part power would have to more than offset the weight penalty of the extra engine hardware. So far there does not appear to be a helicopter mission requirement to drive this development, but in 2020 the situation may be different.

Transmission design is a mature technology with no obvious routes to lighter, more reliable layouts than are available now. If the trend to gas turbine engines with higher specific power output leads to smaller engines with very high-speed output shafts, the difficulties facing the designer of the traditional mechanical transmission will be increased. Such a development may lead to a re-assessment of the electric transmission. Advances in some related technologies may eventually enable gas turbine-driven alternators to supply current to a group of electric motors driving the rotor through a single-stage reduction gearbox. It is anticipated that such a scheme would incorporate far fewer parts resulting in the prospect of improved reliability.

Finally, perhaps the ever-widening use of FADEC will make a major advance in the controlled use of the helicopter engine (and transmission) resulting in longer engine life, reduced maintenance time, greater availability and reduced operating cost.

5.
Materials

The materials used in modern military helicopters are selected for a wide range of desirable properties, principally strength and stiffness. Compared to civil aircraft and helicopters, military rotary-wing aircraft must be capable of surviving impacts from bullets and fragments, as well as providing a potential enemy with the minimum signature for its sensors. The choice of appropriate materials must be made remembering these criteria.

As in the case of fixed wing aircraft there is a need for the materials in military helicopters to be both strong (high yield strength) and stiff (high elastic modulus), while being of low density. In this way airframe masses will be minimised and the payload, endurance and range of the helicopter increased. Traditionally aluminium alloys have been the basis of aircraft construction and any competitor material is likely to have higher strengths and stiffnesses, corrected for density, than standard or advanced aluminium alloys. In recent times there has been an increase in the use of composite materials in aerospace applications, rising to about 10% by mass. It should be noted that if a separate listing were to be made for helicopters, then the proportion of airframe mass made from composites might be greater. An indication that this is the case can be seen by the use of composites in military combat aircraft, both with conventional and vertical take-off and landing, shown in Fig 5.1.

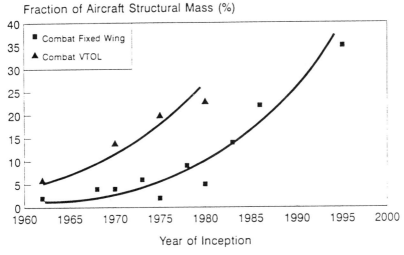

Fig 5.1 Usage of fibre-reinforced composite materials in military aircraft (Reproduced from CJ Peel and PJ Gregson in "High Performance Materials in Aerospace" ed. HM Flower, 1995)

Examples of composite materials include carbon-fibre reinforced polymers, where fibres of graphite are placed in a matrix of either a thermoplastic or thermosetting polymer, and glass-reinforced polymers, where glass fibres are used as the reinforcing material. Fibre reinforced composites may be uni-directional, where all fibres are aligned in the same direction, or laminates, where each layer of the composite may have its fibres aligned in a different direction. Illustrations of each type are shown in Fig 5.2 below.

The strength and stiffness of composites will vary with direction. In general, composites will be strong and stiff in the direction of the fibres, while at right angles to the fibre direction, both strength and stiffness will be similar to that of the matrix. Thus for a unidirectional composite, the modulus and strength can be calculated both in the direction of the fibres and at right angles to this.

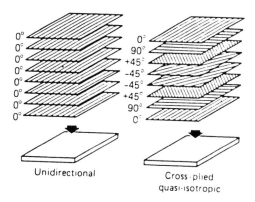

Unidirectional   Cross-plied
                        quasi-isotropic

Fig 5.2 Examples of fibre-reinforced composites

Taking a simple example of a glass fibre-reinforced epoxy resin with a fibre volume fraction of 0.5, fibre modulus = 80 GPa, fibre strength = 3500 MPa, matrix modulus = 5 GPa and matrix strength = 80 MPa, gives the following

Modulus parallel to fibre	42.5 GPa
Modulus perpendicular to fibre	9.4 GPa
Strength parallel to fibre	1790 MPa
Strength perpendicular to fibre	80 MPa

If the tensile strength of a composite is calculated as a function of the angle between the tensile axis and the fibre orientation, it can be seen that the strength (and stiffness) is very sensitive to angle with the great strength and stiffness parallel to the fibre only being retained at angles up to about 5°.

Thus, if the applied stress is in one direction, such as a fishing rod, then unidirectional composites can be used. However, if the stresses are in more than one direction, it will be necessary to use composite laminates with fibres in several directions, a common composite being the quasi-isotropic laminate, which has fibres oriented at 0°, +45°, 90° and -45°. Such a composite will have more isotropic properties, but its strength and stiffness will be much lower than the maximum possible in a unidirectional composite. Typical properties for composites and other potential airframe materials are given in Table 5.1.

Table 5.1

Mechanical Properties of Airframe Materials Corrected for Density

	Elastic Modulus (E) (GPa)	Yield Strength (σ) (MPa)	Density (ρ) (Mg m^{-3})	Specific Stiffness (tension) (E/ρ)	Specific Stiffness (buckling) ($E^{1/3}/\rho$)	Specific Strength (σ/ρ)
Carbon fibre unidirectional	120	1300	1.6	75.0	3.1	810
Carbon* fibre quasi-isotropic	40	400	1.6	25.0	2.1	250
Glass fibre unidirectional	50	1000	1.9	26.3	1.9	530
Glass fibre quasi-isotropic	18	350	1.9	9.5	1.4	180
Aluminium alloy	71	450	2.8	25.3	1.5	160
Aluminium-lithium alloy	79	420	2.6	31.0	1.7	160
Titanium alloy	114	900	4.4	25.7	1.1	200

*Carbon fibre can also be described as graphite fibre

From this it can be seen that, for quasi-isotropic composites, only carbon fibre-reinforced composites will have specific strengths and stiffnesses that are higher than conventional aluminium alloys. For applications where unidirectional composites can be used, there is the additional option to use glass fibre-reinforced polymers.

It should be noted that there are particular problems that arise in composite materials, which are not present in metals. For helicopter applications the most important are: barely visible impact damage, which can arise by dropping an object on to a composite panel or from battle damage, where sub-surface delamination is created; and the absorption of water and other liquids, causing loss of strength and sometimes delamination, if the liquid alternately freezes and melts as the structure changes temperature, particularly due to changes in altitude during flight.

The cost of materials is shown in Fig 5.3. It can be seen that potential airframe materials with superior mechanical properties, such as carbon-fibre reinforced polymers, are more expensive than conventional aluminium alloys. Thus the application of these advanced materials will be more likely in military helicopters which are complex and expensive, with the airframe cost being a small part of the complete system cost. Examples of these would include the Westland Agusta EH101 (Merlin) anti-submarine and transport helicopter and the Boeing AH-64 Apache attack helicopter. The case for the use of expensive advanced materials for a light utility helicopter, such as the Aerospatiale Gazelle, is much less strong. However, as the cost of composite materials falls with their increasing use in non-aerospace applications, it is likely that future military helicopters will have an increasing proportion of their structure manufactured from composite materials.

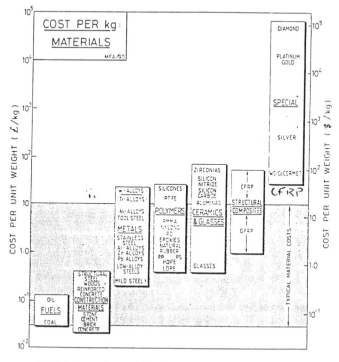

Fig 5.3 Cost of materials (Kluwer Academic Publishers)

It will be useful to examine the importance of materials selection in respect of a series of case studies, covering key helicopter components. These are:

1) Composite rotor blades.

2) Materials for rotor hubs.

3) Airframe materials.

4) Materials for turbine blades.

5) Alloys for gears.

6) Armour materials for protection of crew and essential components.

7) Materials to reduce signature and increase survivability.

Case Study 1 – Composite rotor blades

One of the first applications of fibre-reinforced polymers for helicopter rotors was the replacement of the metal rotor blade of the Westland Sea King in order to increase the fatigue life. There was no effort made to reduce the mass of the blade or to use the presence of the composite material to tailor the design of the rotor to improve the blade aerodynamics.

This change of material increased the fatigue life by a factor of at least 4-5, giving a blade life of at least 12 000 hours, greater than the expected service life of the helicopter. Following that success, the concept of creating composite materials of varying stiffnesses and incorporating these into a rotor blade, which will be designed for maximum lift and minimum drag, was created. Additionally there will not be any restriction of blade shape to a constant section aerofoil along the length of the blade (see Chapter 10). An example of the many different materials used in a modern composite rotor can be seen in the Westland Lynx rotor blade. Although the composite materials will have superior strength and stiffness, compared to metals (Table 5.1), their resistance to erosion by rain, sand and soil is relatively poor. For that reason a titanium anti-erosion strip is fitted. However, this strip will give a clear signal to radar and the strip will be covered with either a thick layer of paint or adhesive tapes that can easily be replaced during routine maintenance. This is an example of the complexity of materials selection, where the simple selection of a material to save weight must be modified in order to cope with other selection criteria, namely erosion resistance and signature reduction.

A view of the cross-section of an experimental rotor blade at Fig 5.4 shows how many different types of composite can be incorporated into a blade in order to optimise rotor performance. The requirements for stiffness are greater near the rotor hub than at the tip and are dealt with by changes of wall thickness along the length of the blade.

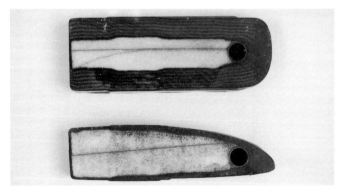

Fig 5.4 Experimental composite rotor blade near hub (above) and tip (below). Note the variation of composite thickness along the length of the blade. (RMCS)

It should be noted that, even for metallic rotor blades it is possible to incorporate honeycomb material into the trailing edge section of the rotor blade. In this way the wall thickness of the blade can be reduced and the overall mass of the blade minimised. This is seen in Fig 5.5 below.

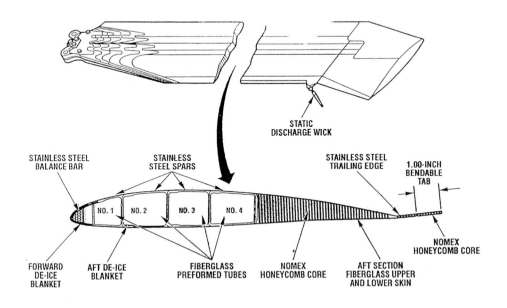

Fig 5.5 Use of composite materials at trailing edge of metal rotor blades
(GKN Westland Helicopters)

Case Study 2 – Materials for rotor hubs (titanium alloys, composites)

Rotor hubs require a material of high strength in order to reduce the mass of the hub, and the alloys of choice have been titanium alloys, typical properties being given in Table 5.1 above. Although steels can be made of comparable specific strength, the overall mass of the hub tends to be higher. Aluminium alloys, because of their lower density, will produce a bulkier hub than titanium.

In order to reduce the mass of the hub, there is an increasing use of carbon-fibre composite materials. For a semi-rigid (hingeless) rotor the central hub will be manufactured in titanium alloy, but the outer hub plates, where the loads are more dominated by centrifugal and shear forces, will be made from graphite-epoxy composites.

The titanium alloys used in semi-rigid (hingeless) rotor hubs tend to allow crack propagation under helicopter operating conditions, due to both fatigue and stress-corrosion. Because of this it is important to be able to detect a crack in service while it is still very small. This is achieved by applying a coloured coating to the alloy, any scratches in which can be easily located.

Some modern light helicopters use a bearingless rotor hub, where control movements are made by elastically bending the rotor head itself. To do this requires a composite material, since the forces needed to produce shape changes in a titanium alloy hub would be too great. However, the volume of the composite hub required to provide sufficient movement to control a heavy helicopter would be considerable, since composite materials tend to be of low density, and, therefore, applications of this technology are mostly in smaller helicopters.

Case Study 3 – Airframe materials (aluminium alloys, composites)

Any change in material for airframes will be based on the reduction of structural mass in order to increase payload or range. Thus candidate materials (Table 5.1) are likely to be those of higher specific strength and stiffness than conventional aluminium alloys, leaving the choice to aluminium-lithium alloys and fibre-reinforced polymers, notably those based on carbon fibres. In the modern EH 101, where light alloys are specified, these are frequently aluminium-lithium alloys. This is because of the reduced density offered by this family of alloys compared to standard aluminium alloys, which rely on copper or zinc as their principal alloying elements.

The advantages of aluminium-lithium alloys over conventional aluminium alloys can be summarised below:

a)   Reduced density and increased stiffness.

b) Can be easily formed in the solution treated state without the need for
    additional heat treatments, as needed for conventional aluminium-
    copper-magnesium alloys.

c) Can be more easily extruded thus making hollow floor beams a possibility
    without the need for adhesive bonding.

d) Can be more easily welded than conventional alloys, although current
    Western practice allows much less scope for welding than is the case in
    Russia.

For the EH 101 the mass saved by the use of aluminium-lithium alloys is 180
kg. However, there are disadvantages that restrict the use of these alloys.

e) To attain the required strength levels for many applications it is
    necessary to cold work the alloy after solution treatment, which is
    restrictive for the designer, especially for forgings.

f) Lithium is expensive and, although the raw metal cost is only a
    proportion of final component cost, this must be set against performance
    increases. Where the mission of the aircraft will be severely compromised
    by the excess airframe mass, then the higher cost will be easier to bear.

An alternative approach to the use of aluminium-lithium alloys is to extend
the use of composite materials to the aircraft skin, frames and stringers.
Referring to Table 5.1, these are likely to be made from carbon-fibre
reinforced polymers. Following from the example of the rotor blade (Case
Study 1) the advantages of using composite materials will be at their greatest
when the airframe has been designed to take advantage of the properties of
the composite material, rather than being a direct copy of the metallic
component. Principal airframe materials for a series of helicopters are shown
in Table 5.2.

Table 5.2

Airframe Materials for a Range of Helicopters

Helicopter	First Flight	Airframe Material
Sikorsky Blackhawk	1974	Aluminium alloy, some use of composites in secondary structures
Boeing Apache	1975	Aluminium alloy, some use of composites in secondary structures
Westland Agusta EH 101	1987	Aluminium-lithium alloy, some

		use of composites, principally in secondary structures
Bell-Boeing Osprey	1989	Extensive use of composite materials, but essentially direct replacement of metal components by composites
Atlas Rooivalk	1990	Aluminium alloy, use of composites in secondary structures
Eurocopter Tiger	1991	Carbon-fibre composite materials, although stub wings have aluminium alloy spars
Boeing-Sikorsky Comanche	1996	Largely composite airframe, designed around a composite box beam with skin panels largely non-load bearing
NH 90	1997	Extensive use of composite materials

As can be seen from Table 5.2, recent designs have increased the proportion of composite materials in the structure. It should be noted that the cost of aerospace composites will remain high, and their use will be most attractive where savings in airframe structure mass can directly lead to increased range, payload or performance.

Case Study 4 – Turbine blades (nickel alloys)

For a helicopter to have a long endurance or range, it is necessary to minimise the cruise specific fuel consumption. As can be seen from Fig 5.6, this is aided by a high turbine entry temperature and a high overall pressure ratio. Turbine entry temperatures are now approaching 1900 K (1627°C) which are well above the melting point of any practical alloys.

The requirements for hot section components are dominated by the need for good creep resistance. Creep is the deformation of materials with stress as a function of time, usually at high temperatures. Over the history of the gas turbine engine the temperature at which alloys can safely be used has increased by 400°C, as can be seen in Fig.5.7. However, the temperatures seen in Fig 5.7 are lower than the turbine entry temperatures shown in Fig 5.6, and it is necessary to cool the blades by means of air bled from the compressor, to ensure first, that they do not melt, and, second, that the metal temperature is reduced to a level where the centrifugal and thermal stresses set up in operation do not cause excessive creep.

The developments in turbine blade materials and manufacturing processes have been in parallel with those in blade cooling technology.

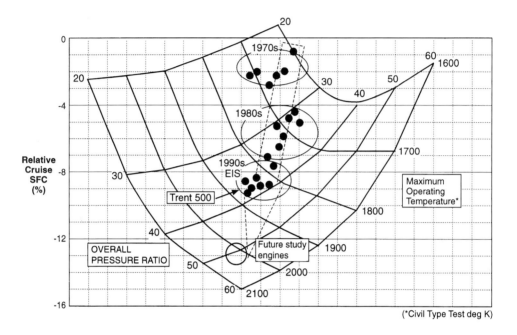

Fig 5.6 Specific Fuel Consumption as function of turbine entry temperature and overall pressure ratio (Rolls Royce Plc)

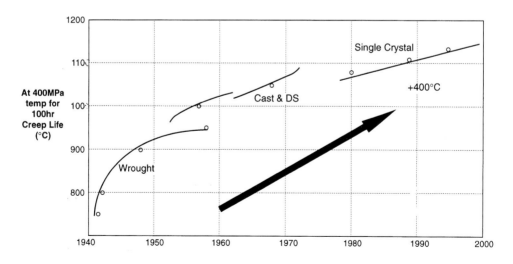

Fig 5.7 Creep performance of families of turbine blade alloys (Rolls Royce Plc)

Alloy Development

In order to achieve the increase in creep performances shown in Fig 5.8, there have been changes in composition from the basic nickel-chromium alloy, strengthened by aluminium and titanium, which was the earliest wrought alloy used for turbine blades. Compositions of typical alloys, grouped in the three families of alloys (wrought, cast and single crystal), are listed in Table 5.3.

Table 5.3

Composition of Nickel-Based Superalloys (wt per cent)

	Ni	C	Cr	Co	W	Mo	Al	Ti	Nb	Other
Wrought nickel-based superalloys										
Nimonic 80	bal	0.06	19.5	1.1			1.3	2.5		
Nimonic 105	bal	0.2	14.5	20.0		5.0	1.2	4.5		
Nimonic 115	bal	0.15	15.0	15.0		3.5	5.0	4.0		
Cast nickel-based superalloys (also used in directionally solidified form)										
IN 100	bal	0.18	10.0	15.0		3.0	5.5	4.7		0.014 B, 0.06 Zr
IN 713	bal	0.12	12.5			4.2	6.1	0.8	2.0	0.012 B. 0.01 Zr
Mar M002	bal	0.15	9.0	10.0		10.0	5.5	1.5		2.5 Ta, 1.5 Hf, 0.015 B, 0.05 Zr
Single crystal nickel-based superalloys										
PWA 1480	bal		10.0	5.0	4.0		5.0	1.5		12.0 Ta
CMX-2	bal	0.005	8.0	4.6	7.9	0.6	5.6	0.9		5.8 Ta, 0.1 Hf, 0.01 Zr
SRR99	bal	0.015	8.5	5.0	9.5		5.5	2.2		2.8 Ta

Alloy development has progressed along the paths described below.

a) Chromium contents have decreased, which has meant that the need to provide coatings to protect against oxidation and hot corrosion by sea salt has increased.

b) The aluminium plus titanium content has steadily increased in order to increase the volume fraction of the strengthening precipitate (γ', $Ni_3(Al, Ti)$).

c) Refractory metals (W, Mo) have been added to increase creep strength at higher temperatures: this, together with the increased volume fraction of γ', has made the alloys unforgeable and therefore required to be casting alloys.

d) Minor element additions (B, Hf, Zr) made to ensure correct grain boundary structure for good creep ductility.

e) For single crystal alloys, elimination of minor elements affecting grain boundary structure as well as additions of very expensive refractory metals (Ta) to ensure a fully heat-treatable microstructure.

Currently even more exotic alloying additions, such as rhenium, are being added to improve the high temperature creep strength. Because all of these alloys will require a coating, yttrium and other reactive elements are also being added to the base alloy to improve the adhesion of the coatings.

Process Development

The earliest turbine blades were solid and manufactured by forging. In order to allow higher turbine entry temperatures blade cooling was introduced, where air was bled from the compressor to cool the turbine blades. With blades that were manufactured by extrusion, which involves the forcing of the hot metal through a die, the only cooling passages that could be constructed were of simple "straight-through" shape with relatively large diameters. These reduced the metal temperatures, but the cooling process could be made more efficient if the cooling passages could be made with an increased surface area to allow faster heat transfer. This is possible if the blades are made by casting. A typical examples of a cooled blade is shown in Fig 5.8. Here the surface area is large and the walls are thin and of known thickness. It should be noted that a series of small holes have been electrochemically machined to provide additional film cooling on the outer surface.

Fig 5.8 Cooling passages in RB211 HP turbine blade (RMCS)

It was recognised that the source of weakness in cast blades was the grain boundary area, especially grain boundaries at right angles to the centrifugal forces acting along the length of the blade. Thus, if these transverse grain boundaries could be eliminated, high temperature mechanical behaviour could be improved. Even better, if all grain boundaries could be removed, mechanical behaviour should improve further. This was the basis of the development of firstly, directional solidification (columnar grain casting), and secondly, single crystal castings.

Once it was recognised that single crystals could be manufactured, new alloys were developed which, because they contained no grain boundary modifying elements, could only be used in single crystal form. Typical compositions are in Table 5.3.

The development of alloys with increased creep resistance has involved the reduction of chromium content and the increase in refractory metal content. Both have tended to decrease the alloy oxidation and hot corrosion resistance. Because of this turbine blades now tend to be coated, as seen in Fig 5.9.

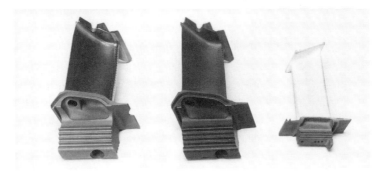

Fig 5.9 Uncoated RB211 HP turbine blade (left), aluminised RB211 HP blade (centre) and experimental MTU turbine blade with thermal barrier coating (right)

The original coatings were created by aluminising, where the blade was surrounded by a powder high in aluminium and aluminium was diffused in by heat treatment. This produced a cheap coating which extended service lives considerably. Later more complex coatings, based on the CoCrAlY (cobalt-chromium-aluminium-yttrium) system, deposited by electron beam evaporation were developed and put into service. Current blades, where the service temperature is high, have a thermal barrier coating, based on zirconium oxide-yttrium oxide deposited on the blade surface by electron beam evaporation. These barrier coatings ensure good oxidation resistance, but have the benefit of reducing the blade temperature by around 100°C, thus making it possible for turbine entry temperatures to be raised. This latter will improve specific fuel consumption, as seen in Fig 5.6 above.

It should be noted that the first stage turbine blades, where the gas temperature is at its highest, will always use a cooled blade. The second stage blades will frequently be uncooled, so as to reduce the volume of air taken from the compressor, and these uncooled blades will frequently run at a higher temperature than the cooled first stage blades.

Ceramics have frequently been forecast to replace metals in the hottest parts of the turbine, but their brittleness has prevented their adoption as monolithic materials. Instead ceramics are playing a vital part in the thick thermal barrier coatings adopted for both turbine blades and combustion chambers.

Case Study 5 – Gear materials (steels)

The challenge in helicopters is the reduction required between the rotation speeds of the powerplant free turbine, which is normally in the range of 20-30000 rev/min, and the main rotor, normally around 250 rev/min. This requires a reduction ratio of around 100:1, as well as the transmission of a large power (2100 kW for the Boeing Apache). In addition, the temperatures of the lubricants are in the range 100-110°C, and, in the future this may rise to 150°C. For military helicopters, which may suffer battle damage, there must also be the ability for the gearbox to survive single excursions at temperatures up to 300°C, which could occur if there is a total loss of lubricant.

The requirements of strength and hardness at the tooth surface, combined with toughness at the tooth core, suggest the use of a low alloy steel, which can be either capable of being carburized or, alternatively, nitrided steel. Typical compositions are in Table 5.4.

Table 5.4

Compositions (wt per cent) of Gear Steels

	C	Mn	P max	S max	Si	Cr	Mo	Ni	Fe	Other
Carburizing steels										
BS S156	0.17	0.31	0.01	0.01	0.26	1.14	0.27	4.07	bal	
AMS 6265	0.16	0.46	0.01	0.10	0.22	1.0		3.29	bal	
Nitriding steels										
32CDV13	0.32	0.48	0.01	0.01	0.33	2.89	0.89	0.07	bal	0.28 V
Advanced carburizing steels										
Vasco X-2M	0.14	0.30	0.03	0.03	0.9	5.0	4.0		bal	1.35 W, 0.45 V

To perform in such a stringent environment, considerable care must be taken with the processing including such processes as melting and heat treatment of the steels. For example, the likelihood of brittle fracture in the gear tooth will be greater in the presence of non-metallic inclusions. These can be removed by vacuum arc re-melting the steel in order to reduce the impurity oxide and sulphide content of the steel, thus increasing the material fracture toughness. Similarly, the risk of fatigue failure arising from the presence of a soft de-carburized layer will be greater if heat treatments take place in the presence of de-carburizing gases, such as carbon dioxide, steam or hydrogen.

For conventional carburizing steels, which have been tempered at 140-160°C, prolonged service at temperatures above 150°C will continue the tempering process and the steel will become softer, and therefore more susceptible to failure by wear and bending fatigue. Since temperatures are likely to increase in future developments, leaving aside the capability for surviving excursions to 300°C after loss of lubricant, there is a case for using advanced carburizing steels in which the tempering reactions are much slower at operating temperatures up to 300°C. These (Table 5.4) include higher molybdenum contents than those of conventional carburizing steels as well as small additions of refractory elements such as tungsten.

Case Study 6 – Armour protection (steel, titanium, ceramics)

There is a need to protect military helicopters by passive armouring, but any parasitic mass will tend to reduce payload or range. Because of this the areas where armouring is considered include the pilot's seat and "capsule" and the transmission around the primary gearbox. Areas where armour could have been expected include the tail rotor drive shaft, a failure of which would be catastrophic, especially at low flight speeds. The threat to be protected against is primarily from fragments, although there is a need to consider protection against bullets from small arms, machine guns and the smaller calibre of cannon.

The best monolithic materials for armour protection will have a high strength and the maximum ductility commensurate with that strength, so that there is both resistance to penetration and absorption of the projectile energy. Since the thickness of the armour is low, there is little danger of gross cracking, even if very hard and strong materials are used. Thus, the candidate materials used (Table 5.5) are low alloy steel, heat treated to a hardness of up to 550-650 Vickers (for comparison rolled homogeneous armour of this thickness has a hardness of around 380 Vickers), or a titanium alloy, similar to that used in the rotor hub. If these thin plate materials are used, then the armour can be incorporated into the airframe, thus being capable of carrying structural loads as well as providing ballistic protection. This is done on the Apache helicopter around the floor of the crew compartment, which is constructed from low alloy steel. Russian helicopters use both titanium alloy and steel to provide armour protection. Titanium alloy is used in the Mi-28 Havoc, while the Mi-24 Hind relies on 5 mm thick armour steel on the front fuselage.

Table 5.5

Candidate Materials for Armour Protection

	Density (Mg m^{-3})	Tensile Strength (MPa)	Yield Strength (MPa)	Fracture Toughness (MPa $\sqrt{m}$)
4340 low alloy steel, tempered at 205°C	7.9	2000	1850	53
Ti-6Al-4V annealed	4.4	950	900	90

It should be noted that, in order to maximise the fracture toughness of the steel at this high strength, the low alloy steel will need to be specially processed to eliminate non-metallic inclusions. Thus melting techniques such as vacuum arc re-melting or electroslag re-melting will need to be used, both of which will add substantially to the cost of the steel. In the same way as for the gear steel (Case Study 5), simple and potentially cheap candidate materials must be expensively processed in order to maximise the useful properties required. If this expensive processing was not used, a less strong low alloy armour steel would be substituted and a thicker section would be required, thus increasing the helicopter structure mass and reducing payload and/or range.

Experience from other armoured fighting vehicles suggests the use of thicker sections of glass or aramid fibre composite material as providing protection against fragments at a lower areal density than by using monolithic aluminium alloy or steel. Thus a shield containing Kevlar and glass fibres in a polymeric matrix is placed between the two crew seats to separate the pilot from the co-pilot/gunner in the Apache helicopter.

For fragments of high kinetic energy, neither monolithic metallic materials nor fibre-reinforced composites can provide protection at low enough mass or thickness. In this case there is a need to use a ceramic tile, frequently made from boron carbide, backed by a fibre-reinforced polymer of high tensile strength and ductility, in order to absorb the energy of the fragment. The best fibres for this will be glass or aramid, carbon being insufficiently ductile. In order to reduce the mass of the armour, there will be a tendency to use relatively thick ceramic tiles and a thinner backing plate. This will also have the benefit of reducing the volume of the armour, since ceramics will have a higher density than fibre-reinforced polymers. Comparing the ceramic-faced armours used in helicopters to those used in armoured fighting vehicles, boron carbide is preferred to the alumina normally selected for armoured fighting vehicles. It is accepted that the harder boron carbide offers better protection than does the less hard alumina and the considerable extra cost can be justified for the helicopter application, since the area to be protected is relatively small and the military and economic value of the helicopter crew very high.

The most heavily armoured Russian helicopter is the Ka-50 Black Shark, which uses 300 kg of armour steel to protect the pilot, fuel tanks, controls and drive trains. It is accepted that the protection could be provided at a lower mass by means of ceramic faced armour, but this concept was rejected because of the perceived threat from multiple strikes. This threat can be minimised by the encapsulation of the ceramic-faced armour, so that the ceramic rubble is in place to erode any second bullet or fragment hitting a particular tile.

Case Study 7 – Materials to reduce signature and increase survivability

It is important to reduce the signature of a helicopter to increase survivability. In respect of detection by radar, the principal methods are to change the shape of the helicopter and to incorporate materials that will tend to absorb radar beams over a wide range of frequencies. Comparing helicopters with similar functions, the radar cross-section of the Boeing Apache attack helicopter is approximately 630 times that of the more modern RAH-66 Boeing Sikorsky Comanche, where reduction of radar cross-section has been regarded as a high priority. At the most simple level, features such as the projections around the rotor hub, as well as the presence of acute corners, will substantially increase the radar cross-section of the aircraft. Thus the best structure for a helicopter will be a load-carrying frame with a skin formed into a shape suitable for deflecting radar beams away from any detector. These complex shapes will be more easily achieved if the skin bears no substantial stresses, and can be made from a wider range of materials, compared to the case where the skin bears a high proportion of the load and must be made from strong and stiff materials.

Considering the interaction of materials with electromagnetic radiation, metals will tend to reflect, thus making metallic airframes easier to detect. Carbon will tend to absorb some incident radiation, thus ensuring that an airframe made from a carbon fibre reinforced polymer matrix will give a smaller radar cross-section than a corresponding metallic airframe.

Under certain circumstances it is useful to incorporate radar absorbing materials (RAM) into a helicopter, accepting that these will not help support the loads applied to the airframe, but will essentially be parasitic mass. These can be based on insulating materials, which can be based on carbon, or on materials which are magnetic and electrical insulators. For volume limited structures, as would normally apply for helicopters, the magnetic materials will be the more attractive. The simplest magnetic material, which is electrically insulating, is iron powder set in a matrix of a non-conducting polymer. Providing there is no path between the iron powder particles this will be electrically insulating, while the magnetic properties can be adjusted by altering the chemical composition and internal structure of the powder. An alternative magnetic material is a ferrite, based on the natural magnetic material lodestone (Fe_3O_4), where alloying additions of other metals are incorporated within the oxide. Since any ferrite is a brittle solid, it will be incorporated into a composite with a polymer matrix. By adjusting the composition and thicknesses of these magnetic RAM layers, it becomes possible to increase the absorption of radar beams over a range of frequencies.

If it is not possible to incorporate complete layers of RAM into a helicopter, radar cross-sections can be reduced somewhat by painting the structure with thick layers of radar absorbing paints or tapes. These will be polymer-based, to ensure that they are electrical insulators, but will have a high loading of radar-absorbing powders, such as iron or a ferrite. These are particularly important in the case of rotor blades, where titanium erosion strips, added to prevent erosion of composite rotors but will increase the signal reflected from the blade.

Any systematic effort to incorporate methods to reduce the radar cross-section will involve penalties in terms of cost and increased structure weight, leading to reduced payload and range. These penalties will be least for helicopters designed with composite frames and with relatively little load carried by the skin, especially if the commitment to low radar cross-section is present from the start of the design process. This is another reason why many newer helicopters are likely to have a higher proportion of composite materials in their airframes, continuing the trend for structural weight saving seen in Table 5.2.

The above analysis assumes that the reduction of radar cross-section will have the effect of increasing helicopter survivability by reducing the range at which the helicopter is detected. If this postponement of radar detection has little or no effect on survivability, then the increased cost and reduced performance will rule out the extensive use of radar absorbing materials. Survivability is dealt with in more detail in Chapter 7.

These case studies show that there is a need to consider the materials of construction carefully in the design of military helicopters. Much of the technology can be derived from the design of military fixed wing aircraft but there will be applications, such as the rotor blade, which are unique to rotary-wing aircraft.

6.
Avionics

Introduction

Avionics is a contraction of the term Aviation Electronics and refers to all the electronics systems installed on an aircraft or helicopter. Historically, these were initially electronic aids installed in the cockpit but now avionics are an integral part of almost all the systems on the vehicle. Some systems can be flight-critical, such that control of the aircraft is lost should the system fail, and these must have reliability and integrity of the highest order. Other systems may assist the crew with navigation or cockpit management or be directly related to the specific military role of the vehicle. The impact of electronics in aviation is wide-ranging and the net result is a new generation of helicopters that are more efficient and more capable in their intended application.

Avionics can account for up to 40% of the total purchase price of a modern combat helicopter, so there is a real need to ensure that the avionics systems installed are effective and appropriate. This chapter looks at a wide range of the application of electronics in a modern military helicopter.

Displays

The pilot has traditionally gathered his information regarding the helicopter state from a wide array of mechanical and electromechanical instruments presented in front of him in a large panel. Increasing helicopter complexity has meant that this presentation format has become troublesome due to the large amount of information being presented at any one time. Modern electronic displays offer the solution of improved display formats together with hiding of non-essential information which reduces instrument clutter and hence pilot workload.

Fig 6.1 Conventional Instrument panel layout *(RMCS)*

For example, a very conventional instrument layout ,such as illustrated in Fig 6.1 can be replaced by a modern primary flight display as illustrated in Fig 6.2. The reduction in clutter is evident together with an increase in readability if the format of the display is well designed. Displays can be multi-function (known unsurprisingly as MFDs), perhaps having several pages which may be viewed one at a time. The pilot can then select between primary flight, engine status, map or radar displays. Having multiple displays increases the amount of information visible and also provides useful redundancy should any display fail.

Fig 6.2 Modern Primary Flight Display (EH 101) *(GKN Westland Helicopters)*

Cockpit Display Technology

Cockpit, or "head-down" displays generally fall into either cathode-ray tube (CRT) or liquid crystal display (LCD) categories.

CRTs operate in the same manner as a conventional television or computer monitor in that a glass tube houses a set of electron guns which fire beams of electrons at a phosphorescent screen. In a colour display, perforated screens ensure that each gun only hits phosphor dots of the appropriate colour (red, green or blue), and hence a colour image is built up by scanning all the guns across the screen in a short period of time. The scanning of the dots is not perceived by the viewer due to the "persistence of vision" effect.

The screen resolution of the CRT is obviously limited by the dot pitch of the screen, and the critical alignment of guns and screen make the CRT a fragile device which needs careful mounting in a high vibration environment. The relatively small angle that the electron beams can be deflected through dictates the size of the tube and this can make the CRT a bulky instrument which requires a lot of depth behind the panel.

LCDs operate on a completely different principle. Ambient light hits a reflective back panel and is then received by the eye. A liquid crystal layer is mounted in front of the panel which is divided into a large number of pixels. By applying a voltage to each pixel, the liquid crystal alters the polarisation of the light passing through it. By combining this with a second polarising layer, the pixel can be made to be opaque on demand. Introducing multiple layers with red, green and blue coloured filters allows a colour display to be constructed.

The LCD is passive in that it only deals in reflected light. This can be overcome to a large degree by backlighting the display, but it is only in recent years that acceptable daylight LCDs have become available. The current trend is now moving away from CRTs towards LCDs since the previous advantages in visibility and resolution of the CRT are being eroded.

Table 6.1

Display Technology Summary

	Advantages	Disadvantages
CRT	• High visibility (actively produces light)	• Fragile
	• Large viewing angle	• Bulky
LCD	• Compact (flat-panel)	• Difficult to manufacture large displays at high resolution
	• Low power	• Small viewing angle

Head-Up Displays (HUD)

Pilots of fighter aircraft have long been supplied with head-up displays HUDs. These consist essentially of a sheet of glass mounted in the pilot's field of view which reflects a CRT display mounted on top of the instrument panel. The net effect is that the pilot sees the display superimposed on his view of the outside world and he does not need to shift his attention and vision to inside the cockpit to gather vital information. The optical elements of a HUD are quite sophisticated and also perform the essential task of collimating the projection. Collimation is the optical trick of presenting the image focused at infinity so the pilot does not have to change his focus in order to read the display.

The HUD has only a small field of view which is more suited to the fighter aircraft role. Recent optical technology has expanded this to a state where a HUD is a useful device in many military helicopter applications.

Helmet-Mounted Displays (HMD)

If the concept of the HUD is miniaturised, then the possibility arises of actually mounting it on the pilot's helmet. Thus it is always in view and is potentially more useful. The information displayed can include video images of the outside world, and this is implemented in the Lockheed-Martin Pilot Night Vision Sensor (PNVS) where an external low-light and infra-red imaging camera system is mounted on a turret slaved to the pilot's head movement, ensuring that the image displayed is correctly synchronised with the outside world view through the sight. The pilot has to remember, however, that his view is from the sight which may be several metres vertically and horizontally removed from his sight-line.

Fig 6.3 PNVS mount on AH-64 Apache *(McDonnell Douglas Helicopter Systems)*

Flight Control

Helicopters have always been difficult to fly, due to a combination of factors. In the hover, the task of positioning over the ground is not dissimilar to that of balancing a marble on a glass plate. The helicopter pilot, however, has the additional difficulty of achieving this balancing trick with a vehicle that has relatively sluggish response characteristics to control inputs. When the vehicle is undergoing any sort of translational flight (forwards, backwards or sideways) then an additional set of difficulties is introduced due to the rotor interaction with the helicopter motion. These interactions are destabilising, and often manifest themselves as cross-coupling characteristics, in that forward motion can induce a lateral (sideways) response and vice-versa.

Under difficult conditions such as low-level, high-speed flight in the Nap-Of-the-Earth (NOE) environment the pilot can quickly become workload-limited. This means that the amount of aggression that can be expressed as aircraft manoeuvring is limited by the pilot's ability to retain full control of the helicopter. Under such circumstances only a small fraction of the helicopter total performance is available to be used by the pilot.

To assist with the pilot workload problem, most modern helicopters are fitted with one or more devices either to improve the handling qualities or provide automatic flight capability.

Stability Augmentation

Many helicopters are fitted with a Stability Augmentation System (SAS). This consists of devices that provide an improvement in handling qualities without affecting the helicopter control characteristics. This is achieved by supplementing the pilot's control inputs with small additional inputs that are proportional to the motion of the helicopter in some way.

A SAS thus comprises:

a. A sensor that measures some aspect of the helicopter motion (usually a gyro to measure pitch, roll or yaw rate, or an accelerometer to measure vertical acceleration)

b. an actuator to provide the control input and

c. a black box to process the sensor signal and drive the actuator.

Additionally there is often a SAS control panel in the cockpit to allow the pilot to disengage the system, or perhaps adjust the gain. By necessity, a SAS has limited control authority (often 10%) to ensure that the helicopter is not endangered if any part of the system should fail.

Autopilots

Autopilots are devices that allow some degree of "hands-off" operation of the helicopter. They are designed to maintain some specified flight variable at a pre-designated value. Typically, an autopilot will have options for speed hold, heading hold and height hold. More advanced autopilots may allow navigation features such as automatic tracking of navigation beacons and waypoints, or automatic hover. Naval helicopters (such as the Westland Sea King) often have autopilot functions which allow automatic transition from forward flight to hover and vice-versa. This is a very useful feature in operations such as sonar dunking, which is often performed at night and in bad weather.

Like the SAS, an autopilot must have limited control authority to allow safe operation of the helicopter should any component fail.

Active Control Technology

Active Control Technology (ACT) is the technical extension of the SAS concept. The ACT system is given full authority over the helicopter controls and the pilot's stick movements are interpreted by the ACT computer as demands on the system for a particular type of motion. The ACT system then decides on the appropriate control movements to make, depending on the data received about the state of the helicopter from multiple sensors.

In its simplest configuration, an ACT system could emulate a conventional mechanical control system but the flexibility offered by the digital ACT computer allows a great deal of versatility in tailoring the helicopter responses. If carefully designed, the ACT system can significantly improve the flying qualities of the vehicle, thus reducing the pilot workload in difficult situations. Carefree handling can be implemented, to help prevent the pilot inadvertently placing the helicopter in a dangerous flight condition.

A full ACT system is an expensive option. All components of the system are flight-critical and thus demand the highest reliability rates. These are usually achieved by triplex or quadruplex redundancy. Many sensors are required for the system to have good information about the state of the helicopter and these must be replicated accordingly.

Navigation

Radio Navigation Aids

Despite the advent of satellite technologies and microminiaturisation of electronics, the aviation world still navigates using radio navigation aids. These are essentially ground-based transmitters from which navigation information can be interpreted by aircraft carrying the appropriate equipment. The systems are well-established and proven, and are employed worldwide, so will continue to be used for many years to come.

Non-Directional Beacons (NDB) and Automatic Direction Finders (ADF)

NDB are the oldest type of navigational aid still in use today. They operate in the 200–400 kHz frequency range. NDB transmitters are inexpensive to install and operate, so instrument approaches based on NDBs are frequently found at relatively small airports with no other navigation aids.

The airborne equipment is an ADF. The terms "NDB approach" and "ADF approach" are often used interchangeably. Just as the needle of a magnetic compass points toward the magnetic north pole, the needle of an ADF points toward the source of the radio signal to which its receiver is tuned. As the aircraft turns, the needle continues to point toward the transmitting antenna. Many ADF indicators have a fixed-card dial with marks every five degrees and numbers at the 0, 90, 180, and 270 degree points; most have dots at 45-degree increments for easy reference.

VHF Omni-Directional Radio (VOR) and Distance Measuring Equipment (DME)

Throughout most of the civilian world the primary electronic navigation aid is the VOR. Aircraft fly routes called "airways" defined by a network of stations. VOR transmitters and receivers operate in the 108.0–117.95 MHz range. The transmitter sends out two signals: a reference phase signal that radiates in all directions and a second, variable-phase signal, that rotates through 360 degrees, like the beam from a lighthouse. Both signals are in phase when the variable signal passes 360 degrees (referenced to magnetic north) and they are 180 degrees out of phase when the rotating signal passes 180 degrees.

The two signals from a VOR transmitter generate 360 lines, like spokes in a wheel. Each line is called a "radial." VOR navigation equipment in an aircraft can determine which of those 360 radials the aircraft is on. The pilot can also select a radial to define a magnetic course towards or away from a VOR station. The VOR equipment displays the aircraft's position to or from the station and left or right of the selected course.

Radio signals in the Very High Frequency (VHF) range are limited to line-of-sight, like FM radio and television broadcasts. This limitation means that hills or other obstacles between the aircraft and a VOR transmitter can block the navigation signal unless it climbs to a higher altitude. A VOR's signal range is also limited. Below about 18000 ft (5.5km), a typical VOR's range is 40–130 nm, depending on terrain and other factors. Above the same height range increases to about 130 nm.

Many VOR are equipped with DME. Stations with both VOR and DME capability are called VOR-DMEs. DME operates in the Ultra High Frequency (UHF) range. Because DME transmissions are paired with their associated VORs, the user doesn't need to know which frequency a given DME uses. Selecting the VOR frequency automatically gives the DME signal. The DME equipment in the aircraft sends a signal to the ground station, which then replies. The equipment in the aircraft converts the interval between the time when it sent the first signal and the receipt of the reply into a distance from the station. If the aircraft is flying directly to or away from the station, it can also use DME to show ground speed and the time required to fly to the station.

DME distances are slant-range distances. That is, they represent the distance from the ground-based transmitter to the airborne equipment, which is the hypotenuse of a triangle. The other two legs are the aircraft's altitude and its distance over the ground from the station. Slant range is always greater than the aircraft's actual distance from the station. For example, at a DME distance of 15 nm, an aircraft might be only 14 nm from the VOR as measured on the ground, depending on its altitude. DME distances become less reliable as an aircraft approaches the DME station.

Tactical Area Navigation (TACAN)

TACAN is a military network of radio navigation aids wholly independent from the civilian set. The TACAN station operates in a similar manner to VOR-DME, giving the pilot magnetic bearing and slant range information, but uses slightly different technology and different frequencies. TACANs are sometimes co-located with a civilian VOR, and are then know as VOR-TAC stations.

Hyperbolic Area Navigation

Hyperbolic Area Navigation is a radio technique for determining position over a wide area, and the systems were originally designed for maritime use. A pair of radio transmitters spaced several hundreds of miles apart emit essentially identical pulsed radio signals. These are necessarily low frequency due to the long distances involved, and are received on the aircraft. The on-board system compares the two signals and determines the time difference between arrival. This then fixes the aircraft to be on an hyperbola between the two stations. Monitoring signals from more than one pair of stations allows a direct position fix to be made.

The most popular Hyperbolic navigation system in use today is Loran-C, but it is rapidly becoming redundant due to the improved accuracy and simplicity of GPS receivers (see below).

Doppler Radar

A Doppler radar system gives an accurate measurement of the helicopter speed over the ground. An array of radar beams is emitted underneath the fuselage and are collected in a receiver after reflecting from the ground. Any relative movement between the emitter and reflector will cause a small change in frequency of the signal due to the Doppler effect. The speed of the vehicle relative to the ground can be deduced from the amount of Doppler effect in each of the beams.

If accurate heading information is known (using a magnetometer for instance), then a computer can calculate distance travelled and keep an accurate track of the aircraft position. This is employed in the Lynx Tactical Area Navigation System (TANS) system, which uses a Doppler sensor. The TANS computer is made more useful by being able to calculate routes to targets and waypoints, and perform a whole host of other navigational tasks.

Inertial Navigation(IN)

The IN system is a "black-box" navigation system which requires no external references except for initial setting-up. The principle employed is simply that of measuring acceleration, from which velocity and displacement may be calculated by numerical integration. Three accelerometers provide data for the aircraft x, y, and z axes. In addition, the system must know the aircraft attitude (pitch, heading and roll angles) in order to compute the correct displacements in earth-centred latitude and longitude. The accelerometer platform is generally fixed relative to the helicopter airframe, and is known as strap-down. Older systems used a gimballed platform in order to allow the accelerometers to remain in a fixed attitude in space while the aircraft manoeuvred around it.

The apparently simple principle of the strapdown IN is bedevilled by technical difficulties. The accelerometers used must have very high precision. For example, if an accelerometer has an error of 0.1 kn/sec acceleration, then after 60 seconds the IN will be wrong by 6 knots in its estimate of the aircraft speed. After one hour, the speed error will be 360 knots. The gyros that measure the attitude must have similar precision and, combined with the complex electronics required to process these precision signals, the net result is that an IN system must be very expensive if it is to achieve any worthwhile accuracy.

Global Positioning

The Global Positioning System (GPS) is now the navigation system of choice for most civilian applications in the air, at sea or ground-based. The system was originally conceived by the US Department of Defense for US military use, but has now been made freely available to civilians and other defence forces.

The principle of GPS is similar to Hyperbolic navigation in that a position fix is made from four or more radio transmitters. The difference with GPS is that the transmitters are located on a constellation of 24 American NavStar satellites orbiting the earth at an altitude of 21300 km. Direct line of sight communication with the satellites is used, which allows a high frequency signal (1.5 Ghz) and a corresponding increase in accuracy. Typical accuracy of 100m is obtained using the coarse acquisition code available to most users. US military users have access to a high precision code which yields a position fix accurate to just a few metres.

GPS receiver technology is rapidly penetrating the civilian market and driving down the costs of equipment. A hand-held GPS receiver for hikers can easily be obtained for less than £200.

A Soviet equivalent to GPS is now becoming available based on the Glonass satellite constellation. Many new receivers are capable of both interpreting both NavStar and Glonass signals and producing improved position fixes.

The degraded accuracy of the coarse acquisition mode is the same for all users interpreting the same satellites. This leads to the ingenious development of Differential GPS which requires a fixed ground station of known latitude and longitude. The ground station receives the GPS position fix, and can then calculate the current error which is transmitted on a VHF radio to any other users in the vicinity. The GPS receiver in an aircraft can then subtract the error to improve its own position accuracy.

Table 6.2

Navigation Aids Technology Summary

	Advantages	Disadvantages
NDB/ADF	• Relative bearing from aircaft	• Relies on civilian station availability
VOR/DME	• Magnetic bearing from station	• Relies on civilian station availability
TACAN	• Magnetic bearing from station	• Relies on military station availability
LORAN-C	• Position fix using passive receiver	• Limited accuracy • Unpredictable lifetime availability
Doppler	• Totally on board, i.e. no dependence on external sources	• Expensive • Non-stealthy. Sensor emits radar in groundward direction • Initial position must be accurately inserted • Modest accuracy
INS	• Good accuracy • Totally on board, i.e. no dependence on external sources	• Expensive • Initial position must be accurately inserted
GPS	• Exceptional accuracy • Lightweight • Cheap • No setting up required	• Relies on US system availability. (May be switched off or jammed)

Databus

All the avionic systems in a helicopter need varying degrees of interconnection. A system such as stability augmentation requires a gyro sensor, a cockpit control panel and connection to actuators. With the proliferation of avionics systems on a modern helicopter this rapidly leads to highly complex wiring. Complicated wiring looms need to be threaded through the aircraft structure and these are vulnerable to damage and difficult to maintain and replace.

The solution is to move towards a digital databus architecture. All the avionics components can be connected to a single wire that traverses the length of the helicopter and each can communicate digitally down the databus. Hence the stability augmentation computer can communicate with its own sensor, and the radar altimeter sensor can communicate with a cockpit display, all down the same wire. Databus controllers manage the communications so that all the separate electronic conversations are inter-leaved and do not interfere with each other. Multiple redundant databuses can be provided for reliability and damage tolerance.

The military standard for aircraft databuses is the Mil-Std 1553 architecture. This was originally implemented in the 1980s and is now getting rather dated. The 1553 operates at a limited data rate of 1 megabit per second which is very slow by modern standards. New technology databus architectures promise gigabit performance using fibre-optic cables which also have the advantage of being immune to electromagnetic disturbances.

Sensors

The pilot of the modern military helicopter is expected to fly both day and night and in adverse weather conditions. The ability of the machine to complete its task under such conditions is of prime importance to the military commander and a helicopter which can operate under 99% of prevailing conditions is obviously much more useful than one with 95% operability. The difference of 4% here can be exploited to win the conflict, if the enemy is unable to operate effectively in situations where friendly helicopters have freedom to roam.

One of the key elements in a day/night/all-weather system is enhanced visual sensors. The eye does not operate well in very dark conditions, and some-times it would be useful to view the world in wavelengths other than optical light. To this end, an array of sensors is available which can considerably enhance the availability of a military helicopter.

Forward Looking Infra-Red (FLIR)

FLIR systems use a sensor not unlike a video camera, but which is sensitive to low frequency light that is not normally visible to the human eye. All matter emits infra-red energy, the frequency of which is dependent only on the temperature of the body. An IR camera is thus directly observing the temperature of the scene. Warm objects (vehicles with running engines, human bodies etc.) appear light and cold bodies (trees, vegetation etc.)

appear dark. The great weakness of FLIR systems is that they can be very limited by fog and rain, when the water particles suspended in the atmosphere are of the same size as the IR wavelength.

Image Intensifiers (II)

II amplifies the visible light received into its sensor to allow viewing in very dark conditions, as low as starlight. Image Intensifiers can be made small enough to fit on the pilot's head, when they are known as Night Vision Goggles (NVG), but more sensitive devices are larger and need to be mounted on the helicopter structure.

Reliability

The most advanced and capable avionics system is no good to anyone if it is broken. Reliability is a high risk with new technology and the issue must be addressed properly to ensure that the effectiveness of the fighting system is not compromised.

Reliability is quantified in terms of Mean Time Between Failures (MTBF) and is usually expressed in flight hours. Desirable MTBF figures should be presented to manufacturers at the start of the procurement process and compliance with these should be demonstrated before the unit is accepted into service. It is all too easy, however, for the procurement authority to over-specify desirable MTBF and it should be recognised that excessively demanding specifications will delay development and add considerably to cost.

The sensible approach to MTBF specification is to ask the question "what are the consequences of the system failing?". The answers will range from a simple "minor inconvenience; mission success not affected" to the catastrophic "helicopter crashes with loss of life and airframe". Clearly the different ends of this spectrum require different MTBF targets.

Typical avionics systems consist of "black boxes" containing circuit boards. These can be expected to have an MTBF expressed in terms of thousands (10^3) of hours. An exceptionally reliable system might have a MTBF of 10000 (10^4) hours. A fly-by-wire system on which the safety of the helicopter depends should have a MTBF of ten million (10^7) hours. A civilian aircraft would expect a MTBF of one thousand million (10^9) hours or better since civilian passengers are not being paid to take risks and civilian aircraft accidents tend to kill larger numbers of people. The large difference between the "black-box" MTBF and the required system MTBF (which can easily be a factor of 10000) is absorbed by the use of multiple redundancy. Triplex, or even quadruplex, copies of all flight control system components can be interconnected to ensure that a working system remains even under a series of component failures.

7.
Survivability

Introduction

As for every other fighting system, the designers of military helicopters have to balance the conflicting requirements of firepower, mobility, protection and, increasingly, information. Unlike land and sea based systems, the fact that the helicopter has to leave the ground to operate and that it does so by generating power through a transmission system of finite power output, means that it is simply not possible for the helicopter to be clad in armour in the same way that land based fighting vehicles are and warships once were. Put crudely, for every kilogram of armour added, a kilogram of fuel, weapons, people or stores has to be taken away if the helicopter is to keep within its maximum all up weight.

At the same time, the combat helicopter and particularly the attack helicopter, has become the high value target on the battlefield. For these reasons, the design team has to create a machine that is difficult to detect, but if detected is difficult to hit, capable of continuing its mission after it has been hit and crashworthy if it is brought down. The resulting design must still be fast, agile and manoeuvrable, is likely to have minimal armouring of only the most critical components and will rely, increasingly, on some form of Defensive Aids Systems (DAS) for protection. In addition, it must retain sufficient thrust margin to be able to lift a useful amount of weapons, stores, people and fuel.

Do not be Seen

Modern and Future Battlespace

In both the USA and UK, the future battlespace is being seen as highly complex and fluid. No longer will war be fought on a linear surface. Rather, the high intensity war would seem to be a series of geographically separate but strategically interlinked campaigns and engagements designed to unbalance the enemy and strike at his centre of gravity. But future wars will not just be fought this way. As the armed forces of the western alliances become evermore technologically advanced, while they will, no doubt act as a conventional deterrent to any aggressor nation from fielding a conventional force, they almost invite a dissimilar or asymmetric response from any aggressor. If it is impossible to take on the US Army, for example, head on, an opponent may be forced to resort to unconventional styles of warfare to achieve his ends. It is arguable in any case that no war fits into either stark definition, but moves to and fro between the extremes of the conflict spectrum.

As with any other fighting system, combat helicopters must be designed to fight and survive the modern high intensity battle. The future battlespace looks like being effectively transparent. Ground and air based sensors, both active and passive, will give future commanders the potential of total visibility of every object within their area of operations. The ground and its topography will no longer afford complete concealment – the idea that a flight of attack helicopters will be able to strike deep into enemy territory without being detected, except against the most ill-equipped opposition, seems inconceivable. An airborne stand-off radar system, flying well behind its own lines, will give the ground commander a real time picture of hostile air activity.

As a result of this potential proliferation of long range surveillance sensors, it would seem to the author that future weapons system designers will have to concentrate far more on signature reduction than hitherto.

Tactical Flying

In order to remain undetected, most tactical flying over land is conducted within the Nap Of the Earth (NOE). At sea, where the surface is, to all intents and purposes, flat, extreme low level flight is the only way to remain beneath the radar and visual horizons. For flight in darkness and poor weather, a variety of systems are employed, ranging from simple passive image intensifying Night Vision Goggles (NVG) and thermal imagers, to more complex emitters – radar altimeters – both downwards and forward looking, weather and fire control radar systems and even scanning laser devices. These active systems will have to be used with increasing judiciousness in the future. At the moment there are very few ESM systems capable of detecting active millimetric wave or laser transmissions, but as these sorts of active systems become more common on such high value targets, so it will become essential to equip forces with the means to detect such transmissions, and thus deny the attackers the benefit of surprise.

Signature Reduction

It is apparent that, to be truly effective, signature reduction must be designed into a platform at the outset, rather than incorporated piecemeal as time passes. Just as the design team must balance the conflicting requirements of firepower, mobility and protection, so it must also balance the reduced signature of the helicopter to ensure a uniform reduction in each distinctive area, as a spike in one signature makes the entire effort wasted.

Thermal

Any object with a temperature above absolute zero radiates infrared (IR) energy. Within the IR part of the EM spectrum, there are, effectively, 3 atmospheric windows of interest:- 1-3, 3-5 and 8-12 micron wavelengths. Components radiate across the entire band, but have peaks within the band that are temperature dependent, which means that they radiate predominantly in one band. The hottest, such as engine components, radiate predominantly in the near IR band (NIR), exhaust gases predominantly in the mid IR band (MIR) and rotor tips and aircraft skin in the far IR band (FIR). Thermal imaging sensors tend to operate in the FIR and IR seekers in modern missiles in the MIR. By intelligent design of exhaust ducts the hot components radiating in NIR can be concealed. Early attempts at cooling the exhaust plume involved ducting the hot gases up into the rotor downwash where the gas is mixed with cool ambient air. Later designs use suppressors that draw in cool air and mix the two within the duct.

Fig 7.1 RAH-66 Comanche *(Boeing)*

The most modern approach is to be seen on the RAH-66 Comanche, which has no conventional exhausts at all. The hot gases are ducted down the tail cone, where they are mixed with ambient air and vented through a slotted aperture. The helicopter is said to have an infrared signature about 95% smaller than the AH-64 Apache. To reduce the FIR image, it is necessary to use low IR emissive materials and paints.

Radar

The notion that "stealth" means "invisible" is fallacious. All military aircraft display some radar cross section (RCS) when illuminated by radar. The amount of energy reflected by such a target depends on a number of variables: shape, size, the angle of the reflecting surface to the transmitter and the nature of the reflecting surface. The aim of reducing the RCS of a helicopter is to attempt to reduce the overall signature, as nearly as possible, to the level of the background clutter and, as a result, to reduce the range at which the helicopter can be detected by a hostile radar. Helicopters typically show at least 2 distinct radar signatures – the body of the helicopter and the rotor blades (and, possibly, the tail rotor). The rotor blades are of particular interest because they will give a return to a Doppler radar even when the helicopter is hovering and, theoretically, invisible to Doppler systems that detect motion.

There are 3 basic radar signature reduction techniques: two are well established and the third is still being developed. The first method is to construct or coat the helicopter with Radar Absorbent Material (RAM). These are typically modern composite materials or paints that can be added to the helicopter in the case of existing types, or used for the actual construction, as is the case with the EH 101 and, more significantly, the RAH-66 Comanche which will be a largely composite helicopter with an RCS 1/630 of Apache.

The second method is scattering: making the radar energy reflect away from the receiver. Clearly, this is far more easily said than done, as it is not possible to achieve total scattering from every angle. Modern fixed wing "stealth" aircraft tend to have a reduced RCS optimised for ground based – upwards looking radars. From above, they have, in all probability, a relatively greater RCS. To achieve a low RCS through scattering requires work to be done at the design stage to shape the aircraft to minimise orthogonal joins and conceal high RCS components such as rotor hubs, weapon stations, undercarriage struts and suchlike.

The final method is a technique known as Active Cancellation. Incoming RF energy is stored in an RF chip and then re-transmitted at half a wave length out of phase, which has the effect of nulling the returning pulse. This only has utility in a highly RCS reduced vehicle, where the radar spikes – for example, along the leading edges of wings, are highly predictable. In such a case, the Active Cancellation transmission need only occur on that known bearing and at an appropriate low power.

Visual

Of all the signatures, the visual is the least important. While the narrow profile of the AH-1 Cobra was revolutionary in 1965, modern attack heli-copters are quite as wide as many utility machines. Glint, a significant problem with shaped cockpit transparencies, can be reduced by using flatter surfaces that do not reflect over such a large arc. Greater reduction in visual signature can be achieved by mounting the surveillance sensors for attack and recce helicopters onto the mast or roof, thus allowing the bulk of the aircraft to remain behind cover. Although only indirectly linked to the visual signature, skidded or wheeled undercarriages are significant because skidded helicopters are difficult to manoeuvre on the ground, whereas wheeled helicopters can be more easily pushed under cover. At sea, a helicopter flying at low level will often be detected first by the flickering of the blades. In recent years a variety of paints have been produced that minimise the contrast between the sea beneath and the turning rotors.

Acoustic

It has been claimed that the acoustic signature of a military helicopter is relatively insignificant because of the high ambient noise on the modern battlefield. In high intensity war this may well be true, but there are many cases where the highly distinctive sound of the helicopter can make the difference between success and failure. Perhaps the most obvious example is at sea – an environment with generally low ambient noise, even on board ships. A naval Lynx helicopter, probing a target at night at low level, can often be detected by ear before it is seen. Land based helicopters conducting covert operations are similarly vulnerable to acoustic detection. It is, in addition, quite possible not only to detect, but also to classify an acoustic detection to a specific type of helicopter. Each has its own distinct signature and at range can provide a far more accurate cue to identification than visual features. As active surveillance systems become more vulnerable on the battlefield, so passive systems will proliferate. There are already capable artillery locating acoustic systems fielded and it seems only a small step to the adaptation of such systems to the detection of helicopters. Indeed, Sweden has developed an anti-helicopter mine that uses an acoustic sensor.

Fig 7.2 The Westland BERP tip blade *(GKN Westland Helicopters)*

The main and tail rotors generate most of the acoustic signature. Rotor noise appears in two forms: Blade Vortex Interaction (BVI) and High Speed Impulse (HSI) noise. BVI results when a blade tip slices through the vortex shed by the preceding blade. This can be reduced by shaping the blade tips as with the Westland BERP or ASP blade: the swept highly angled tip sheds the vortex away from the tip path plane. HSI is caused by the passage of the blades through the air. The effect of this can be reduced by slowing the rotor and by using smart materials to generate more lift from a rotor blade, requiring it to travel less fast. Similar effects occur at the tail rotor and, unless fundamental changes can be made to the rotor, as in the case of the Lynx, in which the tail rotor direction was reversed, making it more efficient and quieter, it would seem that the best option may be to do away with the rotor entirely, as has been done with the NOTAR helicopters produced by McDonnell Douglas (Boeing).

Fig 7.3 Boeing MD Explorer with NOTAR *(Boeing)*

Passive Millimetric

Until very recently, the idea of being a able to produce a real time passive picture of the battlefield at millimetric wave frequencies would have been dismissed as the stuff of fiction. Though millimetric wave surveillance devices are not new, they have been very bulky and have not been capable of generating real time imagery. The great advantage of a passive sensor operating in the millimetric band is the superior penetration through poor weather that is achievable and the comparatively huge temperature contrast between the zenith sky and the natural background (up to 150K, compared to the single degrees contrast sought by IR sensors). The windows currently being exploited are at 35 and 94Ghz, though there are others higher up the spectrum. At present, there are no known mmW signature reduction programmes and it would seem that the only technique might be to use the same broadband radar absorbent materials in use for conventional RCS reduction that mimic the background emissivity and do not act as cold sky reflectors.

Lidar

Even more exotic, but nevertheless technologically possible, is LIDAR detection. LIDARs are laser radars and they can be used to detect the fluctuating or modulated laser radiation scattered from a distant target. A LIDAR system can detect movement in the smallest particles, such as dust and leaves and it is possible to detect the downwash above a concealed rotor disc or the vibrating leaves in the trees in front of a concealed helicopter. It is difficult to conceive a countermeasure to such a sensor.

Active Emitters

In addition to all the above signatures, all military helicopters are fitted with numerous emitters, each of which is detectable and identifiable. Radios, radar altimeters, weather radars, datalinks and fire control and terrain following radars, when transmitting, act as beacons. Until now, helicopters flying within the land battlespace have had the advantage, because EW effort has been focused on communications intelligence, rather than radar ESM. As radar systems proliferate, so will capable ESM systems. It may instructive to look to the maritime battlespace, where radar, though widely fitted to ships, submarines, aircraft and helicopters, is used sparingly and often only as a last resort in a largely passive battle. For example, though fitted with a capable radar with a maximum range of about 50 miles, the naval Lynx relies almost exclusively on its passive sensors to detect and localise targets. The radar is used, where possible, only in the last moments of the mission to engage the target.

Positioning of Sensors

The higher the surveillance sensor is positioned on the helicopter, the less of the aircraft needs to be exposed and the lower the risk of counter detection. Inevitably, the next step would seem to be to generate a surveillance picture from another vehicle and datalink that picture to the helicopter. The notion of pairing UAVs and Attack helicopters is not new and it is certainly worth considering. By flying the UAV to the Area of Interest(AOI) and allowing it to conduct the STA function, transferring the information to the AH or another attack system by datalink will enable the AH to remain undetected for longer. Similarly, the use of systems like ASTOR to downlink a real time picture will allow attack helicopters to close potential targets without revealing their own position by transmitting on their own radar, thus retaining a greater degree of surprise.

Don't be hit

Manoeuvrability

The inherent manoeuvrability and agility of military helicopters has always been a major factor in the survivability equation. The ability of the helicopter to make very high rate manoeuvres and be able, as a result, to take cover behind some obstruction and avoid whatever has been fired adds significantly to its survivability. It is no longer feasible, though, to rely on agility alone to protect the helicopter. Possibly the greatest threat to the AH is posed by simple, visually targeted, man portable , IR homing SAM systems. To counter the IR homing missile there is a real requirement for highly automated DAS, capable of automatically detecting, tracking and either decoying or destroying homing missiles.

Warning Systems

Radar Warning Receivers (RWR)

RWR can appear in a variety of forms, from simple warners that display just the direction from which the radar illumination has come, to complex ESM systems, such as the UK Sky Guardian and the US SIRFC, which display a range of the intercepted radars parameters. Until now, ESM systems have traditionally covered the 1–18 GHz frequency band, but with the advent of millimetric radars and radar altimeters operating at 35 and 94 GHz, new ESM systems will have to include the millimetric part of the spectrum – thus reducing the current advantage of the radar equipped attack helicopter.

Laser Warning Receivers(LWR)

There are 4 types of laser present on the battlefield, all of which are of interest to the military helicopter. The first 2 can be grouped together: the laser designator and range finder. In both cases the systems work by bouncing laser energy off the target. For the range finder, the returning pulse provides the range to the target and for the designator, the bounced and scattered beam is acquired by the seeker on the bomb or missile. Essentially, the result is the same in either case and the aircrew need to be aware that they have been illuminated by a laser that is part of a fire control system. The third is rather different, but still significant. Low power pulsed lasers can be used to detect EO systems. The laser light enters the optics of such a system and is reflected back at the laser because of the cat's eye effect, known as retro-reflection. Many modern battlefield helicopters are fitted with some form of FLIR that allows the helicopter to fly using passive sensors only in adverse weather. The presence of low power scanning lasers has the potential to deny the helicopter its passivity.

The fourth, and perhaps most dangerous, is the laser beam riding missile system. The laser generates a gridded field centred on the target and the missile, equipped with laser receivers looking back at the laser, flies itself into the centre of the field. This guidance system offers greater robustness because guidance information can only be disrupted by jamming the laser transmission. In addition, in the case of a system like the Starstreak HVM, the hypersonic missile has a very short time of flight. The only system weakness is that the laser field must be kept on the target throughout the engagement. If the LWR indicates that the helicopter has been illuminated by such a system, the aircrew can manoeuvre to break lock by taking cover.

Missile Approach Warners (MAW)

MAW are active mmW or passive systems that detect the signature generated by the launch plume of a missile. Modern systems can track more than one plume and can distinguish between threatening and non-threatening tracks. MAW are designed to be part of an integrated DAS, with the detected coarse bearing from the MAW being passed to some fine track sensor to designate and aim an active countermeasures system.

Countermeasures

Active IR Jammers

The first generation active IR countermeasures systems were simple omni-directional xenon beacons – high powered arc lamps that emitted a coded modulated pulse that varied according to the threat missile. While they were believed to have been effective against first generation IR seeking missiles, they delivered low power at the missile seeker (because they were omni-directional), could only decoy one missile type at a time and were only effective against a fairly limited range of threats.

Fig 7.4 First generation active IR jammer (RMCS)

New systems, such as Nemesis, produced by Northrop Grumman and ATIRCM, produced by Lockheed Sanders, use the same principle in a more efficient way. In place of the omni-directional beacon, both new systems use a turreted head incorporating a highly accurate directional IR jammer. At present the light source for the beam is a xenon arc lamp, but there are plans for laser to provide the source in the future. The directionality of the beam gives a very high jam-to-signal ratio that will completely dazzle or even damage the IR seeker in the front of the missile. It is clearly possible, however, that future missile seekers might incorporate a home on jam system that could electronically sample the jamming signal.

Flares

Decoy flares work by seducing the seeker of a missile with a hotter target. While they work well against older generation IR missiles, they are of questionable worth against modern missiles that have multi-spectral, or dual mode seekers. On sensing a bright IR target, some missiles can switch to an UV seeker to continue tracking the helicopter that throws a significant UV shadow, while a flare does not, because of its small size.

Fig 7.5 Flare dispenser fitted to Tailboom *(RMCS)*

At the moment, the only other active systems in service are chaff and IR flares that are dispensed from packs that at the moment tend to be fitted on the tailboom. This is because most chaff and flare systems have come from fixed wing aircraft where flares are ejected astern of the aircraft to seduce the IR missile homing on the exhaust plume. For a helicopter flying at relatively low speed within the NOE, the requirement is for a pattern of flares spread all around the aircraft. A pattern of flares ejected astern of the helicopter in response to a missile fired from ahead will be of little value.

Do not Crash

Selective Protection, Duplication and Redundancy

Armour, even modern complex ceramic armour, is heavy and can only be applied sparingly to military helicopters. Only the most vital, unique systems can be protected with armour and a detailed study of the subject is in Chapter 5. Armoured seats, armoured transparencies and some armoured panelling are all used to some degree to give protection to the aircrew. Modern transparencies offer full protection against limited strikes by 12.7mm ammunition. Duplication within the cockpit of all conventional AH is provided by the tandem seating and duplicated flying controls that allow either crew member to fly the helicopter in the event of the others incapacitation. In the Black Shark KA-50, which is a single seat AH, the aircraft is said to be able to fly itself back to a pre-determined waypoint in the event of the pilot becoming incapacitated. Fuel tanks must be protected for obvious reasons. The risk of explosion if the fuel is released and ignited is high and for that reason self-sealing fuel systems have become more common in recent years. They work by incorporating materials that fill the holes made by penetrating munitions and sealing the tank. There are also high speed fire suppression systems that will activate on sensing projectile strikes.

Traditional gearboxes are very vulnerable to sudden, catastrophic loss of oil. If the high speed input shafts lose their lubrication and cooling, they can overheat and shear. Gearboxes packed with grease tend to be more robust as the lubricating medium is so much more viscous, allowing the transmission to run for sufficient time to recover the helicopter safely. Oddly, the area that is most vulnerable to damage, the tail rotor shaft and transmission, is afforded very little protection. The drive shaft is long and turning at very high speed, making it a finely balanced component, highly susceptible to impact damage.

Single engined helicopters are becoming a rarity on the battlefield. Two engines offer 100% redundancy, even though some performance is usually lost following a single engine failure. Increasingly, engines are mounted far apart, so that the likelihood of a single strike damaging both power plants is minimised. As helicopters have become larger and heavier, so have the control forces felt through the flying controls, to the point that almost all modern helicopters have hydraulic systems that power the main control inputs to the main and tail rotors. Hydraulic systems tend to be duplicated or triplicated because the helicopters are unflyable without servo assistance.

Do not Be Destroyed

A comparatively recent facet of combat has been the unwillingness of the public to accept casualties from their own armed forces. For this reason, a great deal of effort is expended in making helicopters crashworthy. According to current UK crashworthiness design criteria, aircrew must be able to survive a 95th percentile crash: that is to say 95% of all body weights surviving 95% of all crashes. To maximise the prospect of survival, there are a number of design objectives that must be achieved: to maintain a protective shell around the occupants; to make the interior of the shell injury free; to limit the g load on the occupants; to prevent a post crash fire; to allow an immediate escape and, finally, for maritime helicopters, to ensure that the helicopter remains on the surface for long enough for the occupants to escape.

To maintain the protective shell, large mass items must be designed, in the case of the engines to fall away from the fuselage on impact, and in the case of rotor blades to collapse without cutting through the cockpit. Helicopters with very robust undercarriages, like the Apache and naval Lynx, can withstand high impact landings. In the cockpit, modern seats have stroking arms which absorb much of the vertical deceleration of an impact and the seats have 5 point harnesses that constrain the movement of the occupant. Fuel tanks can be constructed of soft, collapsible material and fitted with non-return valves and suction pumps to prevent splitting, rupture and leakage.

Maritime helicopters, in addition to the above, must have some form of flotation system to keep the aircraft on the surface for long enough to allow the occupants to escape. Flotation bags are either built onto the structure, often on the undercarriage sponsons, or fitted for over sea operations, as is done with the Westland Seaking Mk 4.

Ejection systems have been trialled on helicopters. At the moment the only helicopter with an ejection system is the Russian Ka-50 Black Shark. The helicopter has an upwards firing seat and the rotor blades are fitted with explosive bolts that are fired as the first part of the ejection sequence. Some helicopter crews also carry parachutes and in 1996 A 4 man crew successfully escaped by parachute from a pre-production EH-101 after a tail rotor failure at high altitude during a test flight.

Having crashed, it is also important that the helicopter is recoverable and repairable. Battle damage repair is an important aspect of helicopter operations and it is essential that the correct tools and training are available in the front line. With increasing contractorisation of deep maintenance, however, fewer uniformed engineers are able to gain the deep experience required to allow them to carry out often unconventional repairs in the field. The result will probably be that damaged aircraft have to be put into the normal repair loop, making them unavailable to the front line or, that civilian contractors will carry out repairs in the field alongside servicemen.

Conclusion

The concept of survivability in a military helicopter embraces a very wide range of activities and processes. It is apparent that the more the main tenets of the survivability mantra are adopted early in the design cycle, the better equipped the helicopter will be to survive on the modern battlefield, ashore or afloat. Of all the processes perhaps it is signature reduction that requires the most effort. As newer and more exotic sensors come into the order of battle, each exploiting a different part of the electromagnetic, and acoustic/seismic spectra, so the business of balancing the aircraft signature to achieve a similar degree of reduction in every part of the spectrum becomes a highly complex task.

8.
The Helicopter as a Weapon Platform

The arming of helicopters has come a long way since the first Bell 47-G was fitted with light machine guns strapped to the skids. The pilot aimed using grease pencil marks on the cockpit canopy – relying on experience, innate individual skill, and not a little luck, to put rounds into the very general vicinity of the target. Modern helicopter weapon platforms are now complex integrated systems, capable of delivering devastating firepower, with pin-point accuracy at long range.

Superficially, strapping weapons onto a helicopter and firing them at a target seems straightforward. However, even the incorporation of relatively simple waist-mounted machine guns is a complex evolution. In practice, there is a vast range of issues to be considered and it is intended to assess each of these factors, the different armaments involved, the implications of using them and to focus on a few examples of how this has all been achieved in practice.

The Chapter concludes with the arguments for the flexible use of armed utility aircraft, as against the development of attack helicopters, which will be examined in the following chapter.

The Helicopter

It is difficult to conceive a less friendly platform than a helicopter for mounting weapons to. Small and light, it vibrates, flexes, shudders and shakes, is inherently unstable and capable of moving with considerable agility in any, or all, of three planes. Subject to down draughts, gusts and crosswinds, the helicopter needs to be capable of firing from all flight conditions, including in the hover and on the ground. A comparable platform, a naval vessel, at least has the advantage of space, though with less freedom of movement.

Controlling the centre of gravity and overall weight of the helicopter is vital. Adding anything to the aircraft alters every characteristic and requires careful physical and technical assessment. Inevitably, such changes intro-duce new vibrations and stress routes in the aircraft's construction and these can be difficult to predict – therefore subsequent detailed and regular monitoring is required. Aerodynamics can be altered by the addition of wings, pylons, protuberances, outside stores and sensors, with new flow patterns induced. Complex interactions of drag and lift can alter performance markedly.

The efflux of exhausts from rocket, or missile, motors following weapons launch can be highly damaging. The gases themselves are corrosive to the aircraft fuselage and other components. Hot gases, ingested into the engine, can cause peak pressure surges, potentially leading to loss of power, or even engine failure, at a critical moment. Toxic fumes can affect the crew. Blast pressure and debris, such as empty cannon cartridge cases, or the discarded sabots from a missile can cause serious damage. Strikes on the tail rotor system and other control linkages, or ingestion into engine intakes, are a constant risk. Wires from command and guidance systems, paid out by a missile as it flies to the target, can be hazardous. Cannon recoil loads, capable of affecting the helicopters flight profile, also need to be absorbed or dissipated. Alternatively, muzzle velocities must be reduced with consequent diminution of accuracy and target effect.

Stub wings are usually essential for mounting any significant quantity of weapons, although the RAH-66 Comanche overcomes this by mounting weapons within a recessed weapons bay, which is enclosed by doors.

Fig 8.1 RAH-66 Comanche weapons bay (*Boeing Sikorsky*)

Clearly, if stub wings are chosen, they need to be strong and securely fitted. In emergency it must be possible to jettison stores and weapons from the pylons, though not necessarily the wings themselves. Stub wings can assist in providing compound lift. Used in this way, they are particularly effective because lift increases in proportion to the square of the helicopters forward speed, becoming more efficient as speed increases. However, both the visual and radar signature are increased and more drag is induced (e.g. a 0.1 sq. m flat plate results in an approximate loss of 11 s.h.p). This is particularly apparent once weapons are fitted and results in significantly reduced cruise speeds. For example, the Apache's quoted maximum speed is 197 knots, but once a full weapon load is fitted, this drops dramatically to about 140 knots and even less on the Longbow model.

There are other disadvantages to stub wings: their added weight reduces payload and they interrupt the main rotor down wash in the hover, resulting in a loss of lift – a potential problem when attempting to engage targets whilst hovering downwind at maximum All Up Weight (AUW) with low power margins. Relative to ground mounted platforms, helicopter guns will always be less stable and this condition worsens when in the hover, as the helicopter is more sensitive to turbulence and relative wind.

Modern advances in avionics, with increasing use of computing power and in particular greater use of military data standards, has proved significant in easing the integration of different weapons. Software modifications can quickly allow new weapons to be both recognised, and controlled, using common control panels. The weapons pylons and individual munitions communicate with weapons and systems processors, providing details of their natures, states of readiness and technical "health". Fire control, selection of weapon types, and individual natures (allowing, say, mixes of rockets to be individually determined), synchronisation of firing (to allow concurrent operation of different weapons to take place without mutual interference) is all possible. In particular, this also enables rapid, accurate, and often automatic, integration with the target acquisition systems – not just on board, but using digitally burst information from other platforms.

There are penalties. The greater dependence on electronics results in greater vulnerability to Electro-Magnetic Interference (EMI), either from other systems on the helicopter, or from other platforms. Electro-Magnetic Compatibility (EMC) between fighting systems will become increasingly important. In addition to the impact on the weapons themselves, the associated sights, and other sensors may also cause many similar problems, adding to the challenges facing designers. In many cases weapons and associated systems first envisaged and introduced for other (more straightforward) uses on land platforms are being fitted to helicopters.

The result of all this is that the interaction between weapons and helicopters can lead to a mutual degradation in their intrinsic performance. Nevertheless, once these, and similar, factors are understood and appropriate design work undertaken, helicopters are remarkably tolerant in being able to accept a great variety of different weapons and munitions.

Roles and configurations can be changed rapidly. It is, however, essential that any changes are properly examined and tested by the relevant test centres to ensure that the military air-worthiness and functionality of the system is fit for its role. Ultimately operators can be faced with difficult decisions over just how much fighting equipment to incorporate, and as will be seen below, traded for other performance characteristics.

The Weapons

Guns and Cannon.

Guns and cannon were the earliest types of weapons to be used from heli-copters and initially they were simple and straightforward. In Northern Ireland, Army Sioux and Scouts first flew with an Observer armed with an SLR fitted with a special sight that was tethered to the crewman. A round catcher was added to collect the empty cases. These have been long replaced by a series of waist, or pintle, mounted machine guns. Weight (of the weapon, ammunition, mountings, etc), the calibre of the weapon itself, quantities of ammunition carried, empty round catchers – or safe dispensing of the debris – and the sights used, all needed to be considered. Waist-mounted guns are fitted, typically, in peacekeeping operations, or to support helicopters in air-mobile scenarios, usually to provide a minimum level of self-defence. Such waist-mounted guns can be relatively simple, bracketed devices, or can include purpose-built frames, complete with seat firing positions and advanced sighting.

Once larger calibre weapons are required it is necessary either to mount them directly to the aircraft, or particularly in dedicated attack helicopters, to build them, in the case of the AH, into the basic design of the airframe itself.

Options include on-axis gun pods and traversable systems, each with dif-ferent calibres, combinations of systems and natures (including both HE, AP, incendiary and grenade launchers). Guns can be single, or multi-barreled, with either chain, or link feeds. Calibre can vary from 7.62 to 30 mm, but effectiveness, or lethality, of cannon rounds does not necessarily increase with size. Larger rounds can induce greater recoil, leading to decreased launch accuracy, and can be slower and blunter resulting in degraded penetration. Rates of fire vary also. Lockheed Martin's GAU-19/A 0.50" gun can select between 1–2,000 rpm, whilst the Comanche's planned XM-310 (also by Lockheed Martin) can choose 1,500 rpm for air-to-air missions and 750 for ground suppression. Short time of flight is vital in air-to-air combat, or when the helicopter is making crossing engagements, to ensure a high hit probability.

Fig 8.2 KA-50 Cannon *(British Crown Copyright/MOD)*

The KA-50 Black Shark is fitted with the 30 mm 2A-42 cannon taken from the Russian BMP-3, a mechanized infantry combat vehicle. Ammunition is fed from two separate armoured piercing and high explosive containers, selectable according to target. The gun is mounted to the starboard side of the helicopter, and can pivot in elevation from roughly +3 deg to –37 deg and in azimuth from only -2 deg to +9 deg. In effect, this means that the aircraft has to be pointed at the target. Herein lies the problem for helicopters with fixed (or as in the case of the KA-50, semi-fixed) mounts, or gun pods.

Advocates of this approach usually claim that their particular aircraft is sufficiently agile to manoeuvre quickly into an accurate firing position and it is true that a coaxial helicopter is very manoeuvrable in the yaw axis, allowing it to turn, even in high speed forward flight, to face and engage a target, but only, it might be argued, in generally benign conditions. When flying at night, amongst the trees and ground contours, probably at some speed and in formation with friendly aircraft (albeit spaced out), a rapid change to sideways flight to engage a flank target with an on-axis weapon, seems unlikely.

The traversable alternative, mounted in the chin, or below it, sometimes in a turret, has significant advantages. Linked to a Helmet Mounted Sight, the turreted cannon can be slaved the pilot's head movements. The pilot's helmet is tracked within the cockpit by an IR grid. Engagement of flank targets is swift and does not necessarily need the direction of flight to be altered. Multiple engagements, by different members of the crew, can be safely synchronised, enhancing effectiveness and survivability. When fired off-axis, traversable mountings are more prone to destabilizing recoil forces, but improved gun-mountings, fire control systems linked to laser range finding, together with the helmet mounted sights, can lessen these problems, leading to demonstrably better overall performance. Normally, traversable systems have a fail-safe mechanism, which locks the cannon in a fixed forward firing position. On the ground, though, and during landing, care must be taken to ensure that the underslung cannon assembly is not damaged by obstacles, such as rocks and vegetation. Chin mounted systems can be a particular problem in deep snow conditions – especially if the snow freezes around the cannon.

Fig 8.3 Chin mounted cannon *(RMCS)*

Not every helicopter can fit a chin-mounted machine gun. Podded systems that attach to weapon pylons are widely available. The weapon calibre tends to be smaller than chin mounted cannon and magazine capacity is much more limited. The pods have simple aiming mechanisms, sometimes no more than a chinagraph mark on the cockpit in front of the pilot and they tend to be boresighted at relatively short range. For all these limitations, they can be cheap and effective systems, well within the budget of smaller armed forces.

ROCKETS

Unguided, free flight aerial rockets (FFR) have traditionally provided an effective area weapon system, analogous in effect to a light artillery bombardment if used in numbers. Increasingly, improvements to the fire control system, fuzing and launch velocity of rockets are providing greater accuracy. Rocket reliability and performance has also been improved. The increased launch velocity enables the rockets to clear the area of rotor downwash quicker, thus minimising induced inaccuracies. Use of the fire control computer reduces dependence on the pilot's judgement and enables the ballistic trajectory to be more accurately predicted. Range can be increased by either raising the nose of the aircraft and lobbing the rockets, or mechanically altering the elevation of the launchers,. FFR can carry a range of warheads, including either anti-armour, or anti-personnel, sub-munitions, kinetic energy penetrators (flechettes) of different sizes, and red, or white, phosphorous marking smoke. Programmable fusing can detonate barrages of rockets to put up a "wall in space" with flechettes as an air-to-air defence measure. Widely dispersed ground targets can be engaged, with a blanket of multi-purpose sub-munitions placed on the target area (for example, a 400 by 100 metre box at 4,000 metres). Remote fusing dispenses the munitions, which drop vertically at a pre-determined range to maximise accuracy – the range having been achieved by laser ranging. Rocket pods can be designed to various sizes. The Apache 2.75 inch (70 mm) Hydra rocket pod holds either 7 or (on the Apache) 19, whilst the French 68 mm SNEB will be stored in pods of 22 on the Tiger. The Black Shark can carry a total of up to 80 X 80 mm, or 20 X 122-mm rockets. The Russians have also developed 240-mm options. These rockets can be grouped in sub-sets of types, within the pods, and fired selectively, either individually or in various salvo sizes.

Fig 8.4 Rocket pods *(RMCS)*

The Bristol Aerospace General Purpose Flechette warhead has 80 tungsten rod darts, can achieve a range of 6,000 metres (although accuracy diminishes rapidly with increasing range) in 10 seconds and achieve a penetration of one inch of Rolled Homogenous Armour at 1,000 metres (0.25" at 4,300m).

The US Army technology demonstration programme for a low cost, precision kill system is intended to develop a 2.75" (70 mm) guided rocket. Probably using either laser tracking, or beamriding, seekers, it could include one of a number of control options including side thrusters, throttleable valves, or canards to achieve a significant increase in kill probability. This could perhaps be managed for a fifth to a tenth the cost of Hellfire missiles and provide for accurate engagement of discrete, but lower priority targets such as individual soft skinned or lightly armoured vehicles, or bunkers. Footage from the Gulf War displayed the very expensive destruction of such targets using extremely expensive missiles for overkill.

Finally, a good example of the many different alternatives available for weapons stores is the Heavy Machine Gun Pod – Rocket Launcher (HMP-RL), which incorporates a 12.7 mm machine gun pod, with a four round 70 mm rocket launcher.

Missiles

The anti-tank guided missile is the main weapon for many military helicopters – particularly attack versions. The unique ability for the attack helicopter to move fast to an ideal firing position and engage targets at long range, justifies considerable technological investment in an advanced attack system. The missiles need to be individually capable of destroying the most sophisticated of armoured vehicles, protected not only by armour but also, increasingly, some form of automated DAS system.

At present, armour can be attacked in two ways, using either Kinetic Energy (KE) to penetrate the armour, or Chemical Energy(CE). Because of the very high terminal velocity required for a KE penetrator to be effective, launch velocity is extremely high and results in enormous recoil loads that are far too great to be absorbed by an airframe. In consequence, helicopter Anti Tank Guided Weapons (ATGW) all have shaped charge warheads. On initiation, the cone collapses and forms a very high speed jet of material that penetrates armour hydrodynamically. Helicopters can only carry a limited number of missiles of the size necessary to achieve the required degree of penetration. Warheads typically consist of two cone shaped charges, with an optimally shaped tandem configuration to defeat modern reactive armour, either frontally or by Overfly Top Attack (OTA). Precision guidance with effective Electronic Protection Measures (EPM) is essential to achieve the necessary hit and kill probability, ensuring that any DAS system is defeated.

Fig 8.5 Lynx with TOW *(GKN Westland Helicopters)*

Although many older missiles, such as TOW and HOT, will remain in service around the world, more advanced missiles with ranges of 8 km to 12 km are required so that the AH can remain outside the air defence umbrella that might cover an armoured formation. The latest missiles continue to use lasers for guidance, as with the Russian Vikhr (Swirl) AT-9 laser beam rider (Black Shark can carry up to 12 of these supersonic missiles) or the Hellfire II laser homing system. The disadvantage of laser seeking missiles is that the target has to be illuminated for the duration of the engagement. If the helicopter is designating its own targets it must remain exposed to counter-fire for up to 30 seconds. As a result, the more attractive, though far more expensive, alternative is to use fire and forget systems. These allow for multiple, or ripple, launches of missiles without the firing helicopter having to remain locked onto the target throughout the engagement. Having passed the target co-ordinates to the missiles, the helicopter can move to a new firing position as soon as the missiles have launched. Options include the Long-Range Trigat, imaging Infra-Red Charge Coupled Device (IRCCD) , or the radar versions of Hellfire (with either Longbow, or Brimstone seekers).

Trigat is intended for the Tiger attack versions and is cued by the Osiris sight. The crew use the sight to scan the target area, selecting individual targets for engagement and marking them, cueing up to four individual missile seekers (with their narrower field of view) which are then pre-pointed at their specific targets. A probability of "lock on" analysis is then carried out, by the computer, and the crew can decide whether to fire, or not. A salvo of four missiles can be fired in 6 seconds, allowing the aircraft to then remask as each missile flies autonomously towards pre-determined targets. Although the system is passive, it will be vulnerable to IR defensive counters and the maximum range of 8 km is unlikely to be achievable, except in ideal conditions of thermal contrast.

The two radar derivatives of Hellfire operate at different frequencies and in distinct ways. Radar Frequency (RF) Hellfire is cued by the Longbow Radar. The Apache can carry up to 16 Hellfire missiles, though they may not all be the RF version of the missile. Assuming sufficient targets, the missiles can be fired from behind cover (assuming also ground and obstacle clearance for the missile flight path) as fast as it is possible to pull the trigger. Each missile flies to a point in space determined by the Longbow Fire Computer. Depending on the quality of information available from the computer, it will either lock on before or after launch, flying out with its seeker looking for a radar reflection within the target area. It also has an alternate target if the initial one cannot be found. Before launch, targeting information can be passed to it, digitally, from any other Longbow platform.

Fig 8.6 Apache with Hellfire *(McDonnell Douglas Helicopter Systems)*

The Brimstone missile uses the Hellfire body and a radar that transmits at 94 GHz. It is designed to operate autonomously, without dependence on a dedicated target acquisition system. Fired in the direction of a target, it searches a pre-determined box until the radar detects a target that matches one in its stored library, which it then attacks. Possible future developments might include dual mode seekers, allowing greater attack options in the face of increasingly effective target defensive systems.

While ATGW tend to be quite small missiles, their anti-ship counterparts are much larger. Clearly, the targets against which they are designed are bigger, but they are also structured very differently. Warships ceased to use armour for protection in the second world war and, consequently, almost all maritime targets are thin skinned vessels. In place of the anti-tank shaped charge, designed to pierce the dense armour with a jet of plasma, anti-ship missiles tend to have High Explosive blast warheads designed to detonate inside the ship and damage it, though not necessarily destroy or sink it.

Fig 8.7 Lynx firing Sea Skua *(GKN Westland Helicopters)*

In place of armour protection, warships rely for their protection on the sorts of hard and soft kill defence systems described in the previous chapter. As a result, anti-ship missiles are tending to use more than a single homing sensor or signal, so that if one is jammed, the missile can switch to an alternate homing mode or use other techniques to see through jammers or decoys.

In addition to jammers and decoys, some form of air-defence system using guns or missiles or a combination of the two usually protects modern warships. Because the maritime attack helicopter is unable to use its surroundings for cover, it must be able to engage its target from a position outside the range of any ship based air defences. The resulting missile is necessarily large. The Kongsberg Penguin, the anti-ship missile fired by the Sikorsky SH-60B Seahawk, has a range of over 34km and an HE warhead of 120 kg. It uses passive IR to provide terminal homing, having flown to the target using inertial navigation. In The Royal Navy, the Sea Skua missile has been in service since the Falklands War in 1982. Though smaller than the Penguin, it has a range of about 15km and a high explosive blast warhead. Designed to engage smaller targets, like fast patrol boats, it has a semi-active radar homing head, which detects and locks on to the radar echo generated by the Lynx Seaspray radar.

Air To Air

To give the helicopter a level of protection against enemy anti-helicopter aircraft, a number of AA systems are being developed. The first generation are derivatives of ground based, man portable missiles, such as Stinger. While cheap and effective when fired from the ground, they may not be so useful when fitted to a helicopter. They tend to have IR seeker heads with a limited field of view, which is fine when aimed by a man, because he can turn and point the missile at the target easily. When mounted on- axis on a weapon station, the whole helicopter must be manoeuvred to allow the seeker to see its target. In addition, though missiles like Stinger fly at about Mach 2, they are still quite slow and may not be able fly fast enough to engage a fleeting target operating close to the ground in a highly cluttered environment.

Fig 8.8 HVM Starstreak firing from an Apache *(GKN Westland Helicopters)*

To engage the target described above, it may be that a missile such as the hypersonic (Mach 4) Starstreak High Velocity Missile (HVM), is the solution. The missile body carries 3 independent darts that separate from the main body after launch and fly to the target, guided by a laser grid centred on the target. As long as the laser stays locked to the target, the darts are likely to achieve a hit. Flying at about 1200 metres per second, an engagement at 2 km is completed within 2 seconds, hardly enough time for the targeted helicopter to notice that he has been illuminated by a laser, let alone do anything about it.

While HVM seems the ideal system to counter the enemy helicopter, the laser may not be capable of tracking a fast, manoeuvring fixed wing fighter equipped with 'look down shoot down' radar. To counter this threat, it may be that a missile like the Advanced Short Range Air to Air Missile (ASRAAM) is required. Though it uses an imaging IR seeker to home to the target, this hypersonic missile has a seeker eye that can look through 90 degrees and can fire over the shoulder. It can be cued from a helmet-mounted sight, which means that the helicopter does not have to be pointed at the aircraft in order to lock the seeker eye on. Such a highly capable missile would give the battlefield helicopter an enormous AA capability, but at some cost. The missile is heavy, weighing around 100 kg, many times more than a simple missile like Stinger. It would also add significantly to the aircrew workload, because of the requirement to accurately identify potentially hostile targets.

AA missiles are not the only solution. Guns and cannon, particularly chin mounted systems that are aimed by a helmet mounted sight have considerable utility, but are perhaps most useful against targets at close range. At longer ranges and against manoeuvring targets it is extremely unlikely that a cannon system would achieve a hit.

A further solution would be to use an ATGW. While this would cut down the number of different weapons that needed to be carried by the aircraft, there would have to be a degree of compromise over the warhead. The majority of ATGW, as has already been discussed, use a shaped charge warhead in order to achieve armour penetration and behind armour effect. AA missiles tend to use either fragmenting or blast warheads to increase the probability of inflicting damage on a high speed, manoeuvring target. Furthermore, ATGW tend to be, in relative terms, slow missiles which might limit their utility to attacking hovering helicopters only.

Other Weapons

As already discussed, helicopters can be equipped with almost any weapons, with varying success rates, providing weight allows. Although perhaps the simplest weapon to fit, iron bombs have rarely been employed, though depth charges, which are effectively iron bombs with an added hydrostatic fuze, are routinely carried and dropped by maritime helicopters . The Cobra was cleared for their use and the Russians have carried bombs on a number of their platforms. More commonly, grenade launchers have been used extensively, particularly by the US in Vietnam. Similarly, the use of helicopters to lay mines, both anti-personnel and anti-tank has been common, however recent international legislation will prohibit their future use by civilised nations.

Defensive systems, such as chaff and flare dispensers, or illumination rockets, are subject to many of the constraints discussed above, needing to be safely fitted and designed to operate with the same reliability in a demanding environment.

For the future, it would seem likely that greater range, lethality and discrimination will be required. RF and laser Direct Energy Weapons (DEW) are also feasible and target indication lasers have some capability in this respect but at the moment international legislation prohibits their use.

The Weapon System

It will be evident from the foregoing discussion that to be effective, the weapons themselves are only one part of a complex integrated system in the helicopter. Fire control computers, range finders, sensors, target recognition, acquisition and automatic lock on, or auto tracking, systems are all key components. As with any complex integrated weapon system, alignment and boresighting of each system to ensure that they aim at the same point in space, is essential.

Training

Helicopter crews and units require considerable tactical and operational training to enable them to perform their missions. Much of this can be achieved on exercise, or in formal instruction, and as flying hours become evermore expensive, in simulators. These have a major part to play, partly because of the built in capability to permit many permutations of engagements and scenarios. They are also the only place to practice responses to a whole range of emergencies, malfunctions and manoeuvres that cannot be safely simulated in a real helicopter. Traditionally, Full Mission Simulators have been large fixed structures, complete with briefing rooms, computer rooms and control consoles. With newer helicopters like the Apache, there is a need, not only for home based simulators, but also field deployable systems that can be used for mission rehearsal in theatre.

In addition to fixed and deployable systems, most modern helicopters have some on board simulation, allowing aircrew to add realism to training sorties. However, this must be of sufficient fidelity to provide accurate, and relevant, training. Linked via the aircraft databus to its weapon and navigational systems, it is possible to develop effective training packages. These can enable realistic crew operation of the aircraft's weapon and aircraft systems, interacting with other participants (either using data links, or laser stimulation), and recording of all activities for subsequent after action review.

The value of such realistic training is not only applicable to aircrew, but also for other force elements, in training them to deal with helicopter threats. The flight safety implications of subjecting crews to such demanding, exciting and realistic weapons effect simulation should not be overlooked – clearly, appropriate preparatory training and supervision must be requisites.

Just as crucial is the need to train ground crew in realistic support activities, particularly those in Forward Armament & Replenishment Points (FARP) with weapon handling, preparation and loading skills – practised in all day/ night environmental conditions.

While live firing practice provides the ultimate in realistic training, it can be prohibitively expensive to fire warshot ammunition, although training rounds are available, particularly for the less expensive weapon types. It is worth noting, however, that crews training for the Gulf War achieved a 100% improvement in accuracy after using live missiles for training. In addition, finding sufficiently large firing areas to accommodate the ever-increasing weapon ranges, accessible to bases, is increasingly difficult particularly in small, densely populated countries like the UK. Problems are accentuated when lasers, with stringent eye-safety restrictions, are part of the weapons system.

Armed or Attack Helicopters?

There has long been a debate over the need for dedicated attack helicopters in place of armed helicopters. Ultimately, the choice seems to be dictated by the economic capacity of a given force and whether it has sufficient resources to operate both types. In recent Attack Helicopter competitions, the Sikorsky Battle Hawk – perhaps the best example of a modern multi-role armed helicopter, has been included, particularly when the country running the competition already owns utility Black Hawks. The advocates of the armed utility aircraft point to the sheer flexibility of this approach. However, countries will still need to procure sufficient airframes to ensure that enough are always available at the time required to conduct their respective tasks. In addition, maintaining the trained state of the crews will be difficult, particularly since techniques for fighting helicopters require quite different skills from routine utility flying.

Integrating weapons systems into utility aircraft can prove to be just as expensive as in the purpose built options, whilst the weight and space occupied can prevent their employment for utility tasks – removing such systems on an as-required basis can be time consuming and result in a decrease in system reliability. Fundamentally, the old adage "jack of all trades" rings true. Armed aircraft are unlikely to be sufficiently agile and manoeuvrable for the more demanding encounters, particularly air to air, whilst visibility from the cockpits is markedly worse (although sophisticated sensors and displays allowing the crew to look in all directions may lessen this major disadvantage). If a nation can afford to buy a fighting aircraft that can only perform one task, there seems to be no doubt that attack helicopters should be procured, leaving utility helicopters to concentrate on providing flexibility for the many other required roles. If, however, there is only a remote chance that the AH will be required to fight, prudence would seem to point to the armed utility helicopter.

Armed Helicopters

Lynx Mark 8

The Navy version of the Army's Westland Mk 7 armed helicopter is an extremely sophisticated mulit-purpose seaborne helicopter. It is optimised for ASUW and can carry a range of weapons, including the M3M pintle-mount version and Heavy Machinegun Pod (HMP), Sea Skua anti-surface missile (proven in the Falklands and Gulf wars) and, for the ASW role, a range of underwater weapons, including the Stingray torpedo. It can conduct Over the Horizon Targeting (OTHT) for ship launched surface to surface missiles like Harpoon and Exocet.

Fig 8.9 Maritime Attack Helicopter *(GKN Westland Helicopters)*

The Racal Central Tactical System (CTS) integrates the GEC Sea Owl Passive Identification Device (PID) thermal imager, Sea Spray radar and the Orange Crop ESM system to provide a formidable fighting platform in the maritime environment – all capable of being carried on the smallest of naval vessels. In addition to its fighting role, the helicopter is also used extensively for other duties: loadlifting, search and rescue, spotting for naval gunfire, transferring personnel between ships underway and so on. In all probability, the majority of embarked flying hours are expended on a wide range of secondary activities while only a few will be spent in the primary role. That should not be surprising, as it is the versatility of the helicopter that makes it such a useful addition to a warship.

Hind

The Mil Mi-24 "Hind" family, the D and E variants being the most recent and capable, has long been the principal armed helicopter for the different forces of the former Soviet Union and is employed by many other countries. The D version first appeared in Germany in 1975, when its formidable appearance and large weapon capacity concentrated the minds of Western armies. Given the cost of replacement, it is envisaged that the aircraft will be around for many years. It is categorised by the Russians as a Combat Transport helicopter, being able to carry up to eight soldiers internally in addition to its external weapon load. Unlike many Western armed helicopters, which are essentially modified support, or utility, helicopters, The Hind was designed as a fighting machine from the outset. Many might consider that it could just as easily be grouped here with the attack helicopters, however in broadening its function to carry troops (or stores: perhaps spare weapon loads) it inevitably requires greater bulk and reduced manoeuvrability. Nevertheless, it has impressive survivability characteristics, with a titanium rotor hub capable of withstanding 20 mm cannon hits and windscreens designed to resist 20 mm armour piercing shots. It can be fitted with the latest sensors, defensive aids and firepower, although its weapon load is some 25% less than Apache.

Battle Hawk

Of all the armed helicopters flying today, perhaps the most impressive is the S-70 Battle Hawk. With the External Stores Support System (ESSS), which are large weapon carrying stub wings, the helicopter gains 6 weapon stations and can fire a wide variety of weapons, including Hellfire, 70mm rockets, 30mm cannon and 12.7mm machine guns. The helicopter has a higher dash speed than the AH 64D and a significantly greater radius of action. In addition, it can carry its own ground crew and a number of weapon reloads, giving it the ability to remain on task for longer than a conventional attack helicopter. Of course the helicopter is not without some disadvantages, the most significant of which is probably cockpit visibility. This is far more limited than in any tandem seater and can cause problems during flight at low level on NVG.

Fig 8.10 Black Hawk *(Sikorsky)*

Summary

Without doubt, the place of the helicopter on the modern battlefield, ashore and afloat, is assured. No other fighting vehicle is so adaptable and nothing else can carry the range of weapons required in modern warfare. But not all the helicopters on the battlefield will be the traditional jacks of all trades. As a direct result of the success of the AH-64 A Apache in Operation Desert Storm, many nations have decided to include dedicated attack helicopters in their orders of battle. The next chapter will concentrate on this most specialised of modern fighting helicopters.

9.
Attack Helicopters

The US Army was the first to realise the need for dedicated, designed for role, fighting rotorcraft. Chapter 1 has already introduced the Advanced Aerial Fire Support System (AAFSS) concept, but the real catalyst in the development, and subsequent procurement, of attack helicopters, was the Vietnam war. Here the value of helicopter fire support was quickly identified – and equally quickly met, initially by adapting the UH-1 Iroquois to carry air-to-surface rockets and machine guns. It soon became evident that greater performance, with increased payload and reduced vulnerability to ground fire, was needed urgently. The Bell AH 1-G Cobra was the solution.

Fig 9.1 The Bell AH-1 W Super Cobra *(Bell Helicopter Textron)*

Although superficially very different, incorporating the now typical tandem seat arrangement in a new slim line fuselage, with stub wings for carriage of ordnance, it still employed the Iroquois's rotor head, drive train and many other features. Introduced in 1967 with a modest armament, the Cobra soon proved its operational worth, capable of mounting either a pair of turreted 7.62 mm guns (with 4,000 rounds each), or twin M 129 40 mm grenade launchers (with 300 grenades) – or a combination. In addition, it had 4 pylons capable of carrying either 70 mm rockets or additional mini-guns. Soon marine Sea Cobra versions followed and the helicopter became the fore-runner of a large number of "Snake" variants, with operational clearances to deliver almost every conceivable type of ordnance, from iron bombs to the

125

powerful Maverick missile. The US Marine's twin engined AH-1W is the latest production version, but a four bladed rotor system version, the AH-1Z (Viper) is planned for the USMC and export customers. It is not clear whether this will permit the fitting of mast mounted sensors. Anti-armour capability was provided in the mid-1970s by the Hughes TOW anti-tank guided missile, and the Cobra has been sold in large numbers throughout the world.

Whilst the Cobra provided a most effective interim solution, the US still sought a system with greater capability, particularly in 24 hour all-weather operations. The Lockheed Cheyenne won the AAFSS competition and 10 prototypes of this advanced compound helicopter were built. Rising costs, delays, doctrinal uncertainty over the role of attack helicopters, and the appearance of two commercially funded competitors (the S-67 Blackhawk, a Sikorsky S-61 variant, no relation to the current popular utility aircraft of the same name, and the Bell King Cobra), prompted a review. The newcomers were pitched against the Cheyenne in comparative trials in 1972. None met the demanding requirements and the US initiated a new programme for an Advanced Attack Helicopter (AAH). This eventually resulted in a straight competition between the Hughes YAH-64 and the Bell YAH-63 (King Cobra).

Fig 9.2 AH-64A *(McDonnell Douglas Helicopter Company)*

The first of these was to win and evolved into the AH-64 A Apache, the current mainstay of the US Army Aviation's powerful attack capability. Proven in the Gulf War, it is arguably the definitive attack helicopter, against which others should be compared.

Whilst an interesting Anglo-German adaptation of the Westland Lynx, the P277, was stillborn (the UK's laggardly approach has been attributed to both inter-service rivalry and the then prevailing concerns over helicopter survivability), other nations took notice and began their own attack helicopter programmes. These included the Italian Mangusta, the French (initially, but later Franco-German) Tiger and the South African Rooivalk. Russia developed two strikingly different contenders: the Mil 28(Havoc) (similarities to the Apache are striking) and the KA 50/52 Black Shark.

Increased survivability, principally through stealth, sensor technology, sophisticated mission management and situational awareness, are perhaps the core requirements for future attack helicopters. The US Boeing Sikorsky Comanche appears to be setting the pace. Derived from the US Light Helicopter Experimental (LHX) competition, initiated to replace existing fleets of OH-58A Kiowa scouts and AH-1 Cobra light attack helicopters, whilst fulfilling requirements for a light, survivable, lethal, armed reconnaissance helicopter; it is envisaged that Comanche will complement the US Army's Apache. Given the considerable costs and extent of capability overlap, few other nations will have the economy of scale to contemplate such a purchase of both heavy and light attack helicopters. The US Government has given limited approval for some technology demonstrators (a term which hardly seems to do justice to such a potentially impressive fighting platform) to be built, with full production scheduled for around 2015. Sceptics argue that such an industrial commitment will be unlikely and that the Comanche's technology will instead be incorporated into future Apache developments. This is already occurring: an Apache "E" is envisaged, quite clearly benefiting from Comanche technologies.

Apache Longbow

The Boeing AH-64 D Apache Longbow is the vastly improved version of the original "A" model, the latter being in service with many other countries including Israel, Greece, Saudi Arabia, Netherlands and the UAE. Initial plans to develop interim B and C models were scrapped. Instead a rolling programme of minor modifications and improvements was instituted and was followed by the major D-Model modification package. Apache Longbow may look superficially similar, but the new systems produced a very significant upgrade, entailing a comprehensive re-training programme for entire units – using the Apache Training Brigade system at Fort Hood Texas. The most visually obvious difference is the mast mounted Longbow radar, which will be fitted to some two fifths of the US Army's 800 Apaches – limited under current plans for financial reasons. The UK's Army Air Corps is procuring 67 of the Westland Apache variant, but all equipped with the radar, together with many other bespoke differences. The RNLAF is also buying some 30 of the latest Longbow model, although initially without the radar system.

Fig 9.3 Apache Longbow *(McDonnell Douglas Helicopter Company)*

The Longbow radar operates in the 35 GHz band, chosen to provide better visibility through rain, fog and battlefield obscurants than the current FLIR. Its inherent relatively short range is seen as an advantage, helping to minimise the distance at which it can be detected. A narrow beamwidth, together with associated radiation and modulation techniques, is claimed to further reduce the probability of intercept – although any active system is, of course, vulnerable to counter-measures. The radar scans through 360 degrees when searching for airborne targets, but for ground targeting, scan patterns, rates and levels of resolution and arc are selectable. The radar dome, rotating above the main rotor, scans the target area, allowing the aircraft to re-mask whilst stored imagery is assessed – and possibly correlated with electro-optical, or other, information. Colour Multi Purpose Displays (MPD) can show up to 256 targets (selected from the initial analysis of up to 1,026 potential targets) classified as either armour, wheeled vehicles, air defence radar, fast and slow moving aerial targets, or hovering helicopters. Target information is transmitted by digital burst to other members of a fire team. Each team member would normally unmask their radar, conduct a brief narrow band scan, ensuring the most accurate and timely data is received before engagements. Up to 16 radar guided Longbow Hellfire (Radar Frequency (RF) missiles) could be launched by one aircraft, but normally aircraft will carry a mix of weapons. Longbow Hellfire, with either lock on before, or after, fire and forget capability, is designed for use against priority targets – retaining Hellfire II SAL missiles and/or rockets, for attacking easier targets. The entire engagement process could be as brief as 30 seconds, with commanders co-ordinating many units to achieve maximum impact over wide frontages.

The Longbow system is integrated with the Radar Frequency Interferometer (RFI). This antenna is sited just beneath the radar dome to detect emitting air defence radars. If the RFI locates an emitter, the direction and type of the threat is displayed and operators can then select the radar to conduct a narrow beam search, identify the location of the most likely threat and either launch a RF missile, or chose to bypass the danger. This provides the Apache with very powerful autonomous Suppression of Enemy Air Defence (SEAD) capability – and it is important to appreciate that the RF missile continues towards its target, even if the radar to which it is homing switches off. The Longbow system incorporates twin GPS, inertial and Doppler navigation, coupled to air data systems and radar altimeters to provide very accurate positional information.

Other countries are considering either Longbow upgrades to existing fleets of A-models, or new buys. Early reliability concerns, accentuated by spares management problems, were a source of criticism of the A-model. These have been addressed by a range of improvements, including a reduction in the overall numbers of Line Replaceable Units (LRUs – black boxes) – despite the considerable increase in processing capability. Many of these are now accommodated in Extended Forward Avionics Bays (EFABs), easy to access and with improved environmental control. Dual redundant Military Standard-1553 Data Buses provide an effective carrier between the multitude of aircraft systems and the similarly duplicated Weapons and Signal Processors.

But these reliability and technological advances have all been achieved at a price: weight (and thus range). The new Longbow is now significantly heavier than the A-Model. The US Army has partially addressed the need for increased engine power by introducing the General Electric T 701C for radar equipped Longbows (only), whilst the UK has selected the RTM 322. In effect, the aircraft is now transmission limited and, until the complete drive train is updated, a significant proportion of its earlier manoeuvrability has been sacrificed. The US Army has the added operational irritation of having to transfer engines every time it moves a radar between aircraft. Without FADEC, the 701C could be considered to be disadvantaged, with potentially serious torque matching problems. There is some speculation as to whether the US will ultimately procure the RTM engines to match any transmission upgrade.

Once at the forefront of technology, Apache's "First Generation" FLIR now requires modernisation, both for performance and reliability reasons. Survivability equipment and air to air weapons remain developing issues.

Although some warts (albeit, some of which are rather ugly) remain, it would be easy to lose sight of the tremendous capability offered by this aircraft. Greatly improved on an already well tested platform, Apache Longbow is considered to be some 20 times more combat effective than the A- model. This has been borne out by extensive US Army assessment and subsequent analysis by other nations. A combination of multiple sensors, alternative weapons systems, significant payload, reasonable bad weather capability and improving supportability, all make the Apache a formidable weapon system. Coupled to the considerable payload options, is the ability to trade firepower for extensive endurance, whilst still retaining a significant weapon load. Typically, with two Extended Range Fuel Tanks (ERFTs), the Apache can still carry two weapon pods (i.e. 8 Hellfire, or 38 rockets, or a mix) over a Radius of Action (ROA) of 267 kilometres. Alternatively , it can sustain operations for over 2 hours at a ROA of 60 kilometres and these figures rise to some 490 kilometres, or 4.3 hours endurance, if a short running take off is used.

Mangusta

The Italian Agusta A-129 Mangusta (Mongoose) has been a considerable European success story. It is also well proven, most recently in Somalia and Albania on peace keeping operations, where it performed well in difficult conditions, operating principally in the escort role from both land and sea. Although similar to the Apache in principal design features, it is just over half the weight. In essence, it was cost, based on an originally limited and more straightforward anti-tank role, rather than a broader escort and reconnaissance capability, which determined the much lighter configuration (thus constraining payload, weapons – most obviously it lacked a turreted gun – and overall mission equipment). This lack of broader capability resulted in the Italians failing to persuade first Germany, and then later Spain, Netherlands and UK to collaborate. Following valuable experience gained on operations in Somalia, which exposed limitations in roles beyond the limited anti-tank function, and to address the requirements of potential overseas buyers, the Mangusta has now been upgraded to carry much more. The process of this radical improvement is an object lesson in what can be achieved by well programmed modification, building on practical experience. This includes the incorporation of a turreted gun system, based on the Cobra's three barrelled 20 mm Vulcan, Hellfire and Stinger missiles, and FFR. Mission management is greatly improved, with the provision of real time target recording, fire control subsystem, navigation, surveillance, cockpit layout and integration of survivability equipment. This has demanded a significant increase in lift capability, necessitating major changes to the drive train. The number of main rotor blades has been increased from 4 to 5 (incidentally improving vibration characteristics by some 70%) and the rotor head system has been adapted. The main transmission system has been up-rated by 60% to 2,100 shp and the tail rotor drive has similarly been matched, with the increased torque generated demanding a more powerful tail rotor.

Replacement of the original Rolls Royce Gem engines with the FADEC equipped LHTEC T800s, delivering greater power, completes this transformation. The fuselage has had to be altered to accommodate a strengthened nose for the gun turret and stronger landing gear, whilst modifications to the tail boom and the vertical stabiliser have maintained aerodynamic neutrality. Marketed as the "International", or for the Australian competition as the "Scorpion", the Mangusta has matured into a competitive and capable attack helicopter.

Tiger

The French and German Armies plan three variants of the Tiger, with the prospect of future sales elsewhere. Originally a French Aerospatiale initiative it was adopted by Germany, following significant political direction, and is now being developed jointly by Eurocopter France and Eurocopter Germany. In developing the Tiger, three key parameters were set by the French: these included low detectability, maximum weapons efficiency (i.e. effectiveness) and an optimized logistic concept, offering minimum costs of ownership. It is interesting that the Tiger is closer to the Mangusta than to the Apache, in weight and payload, but the French approach has been to develop two variants, support (HAP) and anti-tank (HAC), to address some of the implications of the lighter configuration.

Fig 9.4 Eurocopter Tiger (*Eurocopter*)

This approach derives from the fundamental French view that a multi-purpose (ie heavy) helicopter sacrifices too much agility and manoeuvrability. In air-to-air combat the French see the need for the best possible power to weight ratio, to ensure maximum agility. They also argue that the requirement to tackle both tank and helicopter targets is too demanding, in terms of crew training and operational commitment – they therefore envisage the need to train and select specific crews, optimized for what they consider distinct roles. Germany has however compromised with just one type. All versions are fitted with 2 MTR 390 engines and have a target acquisition sight (Osiris) with imaging infrared, second generation IRCCD, specifically designed to work with the TRIGAT system, a TV camera and direct optic channels. The avionics suite includes colour MPDs and radar/laser warning receivers, missile approach warners, dispensers and other survivability equipment.

The HAP Tiger, sometimes known as the Gerfaut, is an air-to-air combat and fire support helicopter. It is envisaged that it will provide escort and reconnaissance functions to support the HAC Tiger. The HAP is fitted with a 30 mm gun turret, 68 mm sub munition rockets and air-to-air Mistral missiles. It is lighter than the HAC version, to provide the increased agility considered necessary for its air-to-air role, with the sight roof mounted.

The Tiger HAC is an anti-tank helicopter with a mast-mounted sight, with four magnifications, laser range finder, and TV channel, as well as a nose-mounted IRCCD control FLIR for the pilot. Its weapons include the Long Range TRIGAT fire and forget IR imaging missile and/or HOT ant-tank missiles. Some feel that the Osiris sight capability is so greatly in excess of the TRIGAT missile seeker's ability to acquire targets, that there might be a mismatch. However, the passive nature of the sensor, coupled to its demonstrated quality of performance, are significant advantages. Tiger also carries the Mistral air-to-air missile.

The Tiger UHU is very similar to the HAC, but also features 68-mm rockets and a 12.7 mm gun pod, with the capacity for Stinger air-to-air missiles. Essentially it is a compromise which aims to combine the capabilities of both the HAP and HAC in one platform.

At the time of writing a major question mark hangs over the TRIGAT performance and availability to match the Tiger delivery programmes. It may well be that Hellfire Semi-Active Laser (SAL) missiles will ultimately be included in the mission equipment package in which case a laser target marker would also be needed.

Black Shark

The KA-50 evolved from the direct experience of Russian helicopter crews, particularly those operating the Hind in Afghanistan. The helicopter is considered to be a fire support adjunct for supporting, or escorting, ground forces, or as an alternative for long range engagement, with particular emphasis on employment in urban, mountainous and close country. It is particularly valued as an anti-helicopter helicopter. Apart from the utilisation of long range, hard hitting weaponry, the emphasis appears to have been placed on survivability – particularly from engagement at close range by various calibres of small arms fire. The pilot is protected by some 300 kg of steel armour plate (ceramics being discounted as insufficiently robust), with 55mm reinforced glass windscreens (several times greater than the Apaches). A memorable video demonstrated 12.7 mm cannon rounds being fired against this windscreen, with the designer inside the cockpit!

Fig 9.5 KA-50 Black Shark *(British Crown Copyright/MOD)*

However, more striking differences are apparent. It employs two contra-rotating coaxial rotors (each of 3 blades), dispensing with the need for a tail rotor. This novel approach has only previously been seen on utility aircraft – such as the naval Hormone and Helix helicopters. The aerodynamic and engineering arguments are discussed elsewhere, but in operational terms the system offers clear survivability and practical advantages by dispensing with the tail rotor. The aircraft is less vulnerable and can be manoeuvred closer to trees, proving less of a hazard to itself and adjacent units.

It is also argued that the helicopter is faster, due to the greater efficiency of its rotors, and more agile – vital for its air-to-air role, thus compensating for the disadvantages of the on-axis cannon. Indeed high cannon accuracy is claimed, but not substantiated, by the makers. On the other hand, the Black Shark has a higher and distinctive vertical aspect. This is not considered a disadvantage by the Russians, who do not appear to plan to operate the aircraft in the same way as Western forces, the latter incorporating Nap of the Earth (NOE) flying and terrain utilisation – basic field craft – as core to survivability. Instead, the Russians appear to envisage the Hokum as a rotary version of the US A10 Warthog close support aircraft, relying on a combination of stand-off engagement ranges, heavy protective armour and speed, to ensure survivability. Of course, other on-board survivability equipment is also envisaged to complement the basic concept.

Also novel is the approach to crewing. Initially promoted in a single seat configuration, with all the significant ramifications of pilot work overload (particularly in terms of information as more complexity is added) it is now apparent that a two seat variant (the Alligator) is also envisaged. These approaches spawn two distinct issues. Firstly, that of single seat operation. Even the digitally advanced US Comanche envisages the need for two crew operation. The innovative work being done under the US Rotor Pilot Associate (RPA) programme to provide for single seat operation is some way from bearing fruition. A single seat concept for the Russian crew is considered exceptionally demanding, despite the advertised mission management aids, unless the tactical autonomy of the individual crews is intended to be very limited. The other issue is the side by side configuration of the two man version. This does allow the height of the fuselage itself (ignoring the height of the twin rotor system) to be compressed, albeit at the expense of widening the cockpit. Hitherto, this was not considered attractive to Western designers, hence the common tandem configuration, since it restricted the ability of individual crew members to scan from left to right unhindered – a major disadvantage highlighted in the earlier discussion on armed versus dedicated attack helicopters. However, with the advent of improved sensor packages, mounted externally, and sophisticated integration of these different sensors into helmet mounted displays, it is perhaps feasible to see some disadvantages being overcome – in effect each crewman will be able to "look through" his partner and/or the aircraft itself, at will. Additionally they will be able to see exactly what co-pilots are up to in the cockpit itself, a shortfall in tandem configurations.

Perhaps the most dramatic innovation is the crew ejection system. Various types of systems have been postulated for other aircraft, but never implemented. The approach is based on the Zveda K-37 rocket-powered pilot escape system, and initially developed for the Russian VSTOL fighter, the YAK-141. The integrated system envisages a sequence of blade jettison, followed by rocket propulsion of the crew seat assembly through the cockpit roof; separation of the crew from the assembly and parachute deployment to arrest descent. Whilst this approach has been demonstrated from a variety of air speeds and aircraft attitudes, critics claim the blades pose a major threat to other accompanying aircraft (with a probability of a strike at 35% at a separation of some 160 feet).

It is also of note that increasing use is being made of Western technology for the Man Machine Interface (MMI), displays, mission management and sensors. Bespoke packages are available for potential buyers, potentially making this robust, heavily engineered aircraft a very attractive alternative to more conventional attack helicopters. The arguments between Havoc (not discussed here) and Black Shark are likely to continue to rage in Russian circles, as each claims relative advantages over the other. It is worth bearing in mind that the Black Shark did apparently beat the Havoc, itself considered to be a well designed and extremely effective battlefield system, in a competitive field trial, conducted by battle hardened Russian aircrew.

Rooivalk

The South African Denel Rooivalk (Red Hawk) was developed in direct response to the Angolan conflict, where the need for robust, rugged attack capability was determined. The design is based on the Puma, which is built under licence as the Oryx and the two helicopters share many parts. Its entry into the competitive market was initially for the UK requirement, where the South Africans gained valuable commercial experience. At the time the political situation was still uncertain and apparent US reluctance to transfer the requisite technology meant that this potentially interesting solution did not make the final selection. Very similar to the Apache in size and concept, but without a mast-mounted sensor, its early development model quickly demonstrated a reputation for exemplary availability. With the appropriate mission equipment package it is now seen as a serious commercial contender. The SAAF have ordered 12 aircraft, all scheduled for delivery by 2001.

XOH-1

At the time of writing, little is known of Japan's XOH-1 programme for an all-Japanese developed scout helicopter, which had its initial roll out in 1996. Equipped with a thermal imager, TV camera and laser range finder, it is scheduled to have self-defence Air to Air Missiles with hard points for extended range fuel tanks. It purports to have a relatively light non-offensive role. Nevertheless, it does have hard points for other munitions and could provide an indigenous solution for Asian markets seeking a cheap, light attack helicopter. The Japanese Ground Self Defence Force plans to introduce up to 250 aircraft from the year 2000 onwards.

Fig 9.6 Kawasaki XOH-1 *(Kawasaki Heavy Industries Ltd)*

Comanche

The primary mission of the Boeing-Sikorsky Reconnaissance Attack Helicopter (RAH)-66 Comanche is reconnaissance. Smaller and lighter than the Apache, with second generation optics and a reduced signature, it is designed to both see further and get closer to targets, without detection, increasing mission performance and survivability. It is envisaged that the thermal imager will see about 50% further than the current Apache TADS, in fog and rain, and identify targets at twice the distance. Currently two prototype and five Early Operational Capability (EOC) aircraft are planned, to give an initial EOC in 2006, with decisions on full production deferred into the following decade.

Designed for stealth, it has a shrouded tail rotor, a shaped fuselage to reduce radar cross section, a very narrow frontal aspect and weapon carriage points in bays which open when required, reducing both drag and signature (options allow these to be fully deployed to carry more armaments, if required). A low glint canopy, IR suppressant paint and materials, and both passive and active counter measures are all incorporated to assist in reducing the overall signature. Longbow radar is desired, but the overall programme has been dogged by weight problems and the final solution is unclear. Considerable effort is devoted towards glass cockpit integration and there is no doubt that technology will flow between the RPA, Comanche and Apache programmes.

Fig 9.7 RAH-66 Comanche on an early test flight *(Boeing)*

Maritime

The majority of typical maritime tasks lend themselves to the "armed" approach discussed in the previous chapter. However, in amphibious operation scenarios, as well as in the littoral, the need for an attack helicopter capability has also been identified – albeit with targets including surface shipping. In the US Navy and Marines these needs have been met by the Cobra variants, currently the AH-1W model. A SeaApache was mooted at one point, possibly as a replacement for the Cobra, but it quickly became apparent that this would be too expensive, particularly once bespoke maritime requirements were incorporated – and taking into account the vast numbers of Cobras which would need replacement.

In effect, the trend in nations has been to take its land attack helicopter and adapt it the marine environment, developing procedures to accommodate problems. The UK's approach has been illustrative of some of the difficulties which prevail. During the competition to select a UK attack helicopter, the GEC Bell consortium promoted Cobra Venom (a Whisky model variant, although at a late stage a 4 bladed version was proffered) argued that this would, as the only proven "marinised" aircraft being offered, provide significant advantage. This side stepped the reality that the heavily adapted Venom was, in effect, a very different aircraft from existing Cobras, particularly in the vital areas of electronics. Ultimately the decision rested on other critical areas and the UK was faced with separately addressing the maritime implications of the selected WAH 64 Apache.

A purpose built derivative, incorporating deck landing gear and fully "marinised" aircraft systems would be prohibitively costly, but there is a need to ensure that electronics, from both munition and flight safety aspects, are safe from radiation hazards. Apocryphal stories of US Apache "A" models, jacking themselves up by their cannons – caused by spurious emissions generating gun articulation signals – are demonstrable examples of the risks entailed. As a result, appropriate (ie. intensive) testing of the aircraft and its systems is planned – a must for any operator intending to put aircraft into the extreme radiation environment which prevails on board ships. Other issues, such as the need for procedures to reduce salt corrosion and for deck handling of the rather large and ungainly (particularly with its higher centre of gravity) Apache will need to be dealt with in a pragmatic and cost-effective manner. The need for communications (and information systems as a whole) interoperability, together with appropriate training, is evident. The subject of marinisation has been covered in more detail in Chapter 2.

Summary

Attack helicopters have the potential to impact significantly on battlefields, for the foreseeable future. Increasingly, they are likely to be pitted against each other. They will have to develop continually if they are to retain technological superiority over traditional threats. This will demand considerable investment and cost-effective analysis of future options will inevitably be sharply focused. The durability of the attack helicopter's current pre-eminence is finite and their use will be adapted. Lighter, stealthier (either manned, or un-manned) sensor platforms, teamed to cue heavier, less survivable, weapons carriers providing longer-range indirect fire, can already be envisaged. In the meantime, increasingly powerful forces of attack helicopters are being introduced world-wide, with older tried and trusted aircraft, such as the Cobra, being built in large numbers under licence.

10
Future Trends

Introduction

While any discussion of future trends is necessarily highly speculative, there seem to be a number of significant indicators as to the way in which the future battle might be fought and the types of rotorcraft that might be operating. Modern attack helicopters like the AH-64 Apache Longbow and the radar-equipped Ka-52 Alligator represent the acme of their type at the time of writing but it would appear that future systems may be very different, due to three factors.

The first factor is speed. Conventional helicopters remain limited to a top speed of about 200 knots (370 km/h). While this is more than adequate today, the very high tempo of operations envisaged by the USA's Army After Next (AAN) project will make it essential for helicopters to fly faster if they are to keep up with the battle. The second factor is the distinctive signatures of the helicopter – acoustic, thermal, radar, and passive. Signature management and signature reduction are areas of technology largely new to land forces. Until very recently, the land battlefield has been, in relative terms, electronically clean and battles fought largely without the benefit of sophisticated sensors like radar and IR scanners. There has been a recent proliferation of sensors on the battlefield and while radar has given armies the ability to see at night and in fog, its inherent vulnerability as an active system leads one to speculate that it will be, with one marked exception, passive systems that will predominate in the next few years. The third, and final factor, is that helicopters still do not have a true 24-hour capability. At best they are adverse weather capable. Fog is and will remain impenetrable to IR imagers, the current preferred sensor. If commanders wish to conduct their Manoeuvre operations at 0400 on a dark foggy morning then they will be without helicopter support.

Improving Maximum Speed

Conventional helicopters are currently limited to a maximum speed of about 200 knots (370 km/h) but are generally optimised to cruise at speeds between 120 and 150 knots (220–280 km/h) and fly safely in the nap of the earth at about 45 knots (85 km/h). With the increase in operational tempo to around 110 knots (around 200 km/h) conventional helicopters, operating in the nap of the earth will be unable to keep pace with the battle, let alone lead it. There appear to be three generic ways of raising the speed of the helicopter above 200 knots: rotor tip modifications, the Advancing Blade Concept (ABC) and Compounding. These will be discussed in the following sub-sections, together with various forms of convertiplanes, which get round the helicopter's inherent speed limitations by converting to some form of fixed wing aircraft for high-speed flight.

Rotor Tip Modifications

It was shown in Chapter 3 that the helicopter rotor suffers from two conflicting aerodynamic problems at high forward speed: advancing blade compressibility and retreating blade stall. "Compressibility" here refers to the tendency of the air to be compressed due to the high Mach number (air speed relative to atmospheric speed of sound) near the tip of the advancing blade. This high relative Mach number in turn leads to the formation of shock waves on the blade, causing high drag, increased noise and vibration and possible loss of lift. The traditional aerodynamic solution to compressibility problems is to use wing sweep and increasingly helicopter designers are introducing swept tips to reduce the strength of the shock waves on the advancing tip. Most designs, however, can only incorporate quite modest levels of tip sweep because of the nose-down twisting which is induced in the rotor blade by lift at the tip acting behind the main spar. Thus, tip sweep is currently limited, on many designs, by blade structural considerations and is not used to produce high forward speeds.

During the 1980s, however, the British Experimental Rotor Programme (BERP) led to the design of a modified tip that had a high level of sweep-back. To overcome the blade twisting problems the swept tip was displaced forward so that its lift acted in line with the main spar. This produced a large kink in the leading edge of the blade, which turned out to have a beneficial effect on the retreating side of the rotor, where the angles of attack are high. This so-called BERP tip operates like a delta wing at high angles of attack: it generates a powerful vortex above the blade upper surface and this in turn generates lift which continues to increase up to very high angles of attack. At the same time, the high tip sweep has allowed the advancing blade to be operated at high relative Mach numbers. Overall, a dramatic increase in rotor thrust, of the order of 40%, was possible and in August 1986 a Lynx helicopter fitted with BERP blades raised the World Helicopter Speed record to 400.87km/h (about 216 knots). It should be noted that further modifications were also required to the helicopter to achieve this record. Extra vertical tail surfaces had to be fitted to generate an aerodynamic side-force and off-load the tail rotor which was otherwise suffering from its own aerodynamic problems under the high speed and high power conditions. The engines and gearbox also had to be up-rated (by about 5%) and the exhausts were modified so that some jet thrust was achieved.

Fig 10.1 Westland G – Lynx (GKN Westland Helicopters)

This last point will be discussed further below under "Compounding". Finally, it should be noted that the complex aerodynamic design of the Westland "BERP" tip can only be realised in practice through the use of composite materials and manufacturing techniques.

Advancing Blade Concept

Since a single rotor suffers a tendency to roll due to the asymmetry between its advancing and retreating sides in forward flight, it would seem that two such rotors mounted co-axially and contra-rotating would solve this problem. This would only work, however, if the blades were not fitted with flapping hinges, since these act automatically to balance the forward flight asymmetry on each rotor. A co-axial rotor with rigid blades has flown on the Sikorsky XH-59A (or S-69) ABC (Advancing Blade Concept) demonstrator. Each rotor disc was able to generate all the lift available on the advancing side, with the rolling tendency of one rotor disc cancelling out that from the other; the retreating blades could be set at reduced incidence to avoid stall. In principle this configuration allows high forward speeds, in excess of 230 knots (425 km/h) and high agility thanks to the rigid rotor and high available thrust levels.

Sikorsky demonstrated speeds in excess of 260 knots (480 km/h) using the ABC aircraft fitted with two jet engines for extra thrust. As a pure helicopter there appear to be some problems with the ABC concept. One of these may be a vibration problem associated with the rigid rotors. Another limitation may be due to the fact that the retreating blade is generating less drag than normal; this drag acts towards the front of the aircraft and contributes to the forward thrust. Whatever the technical reasons, the ABC demonstrator appears to have ended its flying programme and there have been no recent proposals for future rotorcraft based on this concept.

Compounding

An alternative approach to the limitations imposed by forward flight lift asymmetry is to off-load the rotor by adding fixed wings and/or propulsive engines; an approach known as Compounding. Fixed wings help to reduce the retreating blade stall limitations by allowing the rotor to be operated at lower angles of attack. On its own this so-called Lift Compounding does not allow higher forward speeds (unless the aircraft is power-limited). Higher speeds can be achieved through Thrust Compounding, which requires the addition of propulsive engines (jets or propellers).

Numerous research programmes over the last 30 years have developed a variety of Compound helicopters. Many of these merely added jet engines to existing helicopters and demonstrated higher speeds than for the pure helicopter but accompanied by higher fuel consumption. A few, however, were designed from the outset as Compound aircraft. Most notable amongst these, from the military point of view, was the Lockheed AH-56 Cheyenne. This featured a moderately large fixed wing, a pusher propeller and a very rigid main rotor. By slowing the rotor down to avoid compressibility problems such a configuration should be capable of about 350 knots (650 km/h).

The Cheyenne demonstrated the high-speed capability of the compound helicopter, but it also revealed some problems with certain design features. Its pusher propeller was very close to the conventional tail rotor and the two rotors would try to use the same airflow, producing an unsteady yawing behaviour. This problem could be overcome in a future Compound helicopter by using a single ducted rotor with vectoring vanes, to produce both thrust and torque reaction (although this can have limitations for sideways flight). Other development problems were associated with the rigid main rotor. This gave the helicopter an exceptional level of manoeuvrability but also produced vibration and stability problems. These could be overcome with current levels of technology and understanding.

Westland Helicopters and Rolls-Royce have recently proposed an interesting scheme for an advanced compound helicopter. This was based on their experience with the Lynx during its World Helicopter Speed attempt. Their proposal features a Lynx airframe (for demonstration purposes) with a fixed wing and jet thrust achieved by fitting variable-area nozzles to the engine exhausts. This latter feature allows a smooth variation between rotor and jet propelled flight. The nozzle area would be increased at low speeds giving little jet thrust and most engine power to the rotor. At high speeds the nozzle area would be reduced giving increased jet thrust but at the same time reducing the power output from the turbine thus reducing rotor power. An additional advantage of thrust compounding, besides the direct contribution to forward thrust, is the reduction in parasite drag. This occurs because high forward speeds can be achieved at a less nose-down incidence and this reduces the drag of the fuselage.

Convertiplanes

The term "convertiplane" covers a variety of configurations that attempt to combine the advantages of the helicopter (efficient hover, good low-speed manoeuvrability) with those of the aeroplane (high flight speed, long range). The basic approach in these concepts is to remove the edge-wise rotor for high-speed flight, by converting it either into a propeller or into a fixed wing.

Tilt-rotor

Bell and Boeing have adopted the former approach with the V-22 Osprey. This is a tilt-rotor, where two rotors are mounted at the ends of a fixed wing and, together with their respective engines, can be tilted to form either helicopter rotors or propellers. This concept, together with the similar tilt-wing, has been around for several decades but has required the combination of several technologies (composite materials, computational aerodynamic design, vibration reduction) to produce a feasible production aircraft.

The tilt-rotor is, inevitably, a compromise design. The rotors are rather small for efficient helicopter-like hover (giving high disc loading and, consequently, high downwash velocities, which can be an issue for ground personnel during underslung load work) but rather large as propellers for very high speed flight. (A possible scheme has been proposed to solve this, involving telescopic rotor blades to change disc loading between propeller and helicopter modes.) In the hover the rotor wake impinges on the wing giving a large down force which reduces the effective payload; this has to be offset by extensive use of composites to save weight. Nevertheless, the Osprey appears to offer the advantages of both rotary and fixed wing vehicles, giving the aircraft a generous low speed flight envelope and a high transit speed. It is the high-speed conventional transit that will transform the way in which amphibious operations in particular are conducted. At present the relatively slow speed of most utility helicopters means that the amphibious group must assault from a position close to the coast. With the V-22, the assault can be conducted from well over the horizon, far from the eyes and weapons of the enemy.

Fig 10.2 V-22 Osprey *(Boeing)*

X-wing

If a helicopter's rotor could be stopped for high-speed flight then its limitations would cease to be a problem. To achieve this, however, the rotor blades would have to be as rigid and large as fixed wings (since centrifugal force would not be available to "stiffen" them) and some means would have to be found to switch the position of the trailing edge between rotor-borne and wing-borne flight. A separate means of thrust generation would, of course, be required. NASA and Sikorsky proposed such a scheme, known as the X-wing, during the 1980s.

The rotor featured "circulation control", whereby compressed air could be blown from the trailing edge of an elliptical-section aerofoil to control the lift. This is the same principle as is used in the NOTAR tail boom and, in the case of X-wing, allows the trailing edge of the rotor blade to be swapped by changing the position of the blowing. In principle, this scheme allows supersonic speeds to be achieved in fixed-wing mode if suitable jet propulsion were used. In practice, the complexity of the "plumbing" required to distribute the circulation control blowing during transition from rotary- to fixed-wing flight has proved excessive. The X-wing programme did not receive funding to proceed to flight test.

Canard Rotor/Wing

An alternative method to the X-wing is that being adopted by Boeing in their Canard Rotor/Wing project. Below about 120 knots (about 220 km/h) the aircraft flies like a helicopter, with lift and directional thrust generated by the two-bladed rotor. This rotor employs circulation control and is driven by jet reaction, removing the need for a tail rotor. As the aircraft speed increases to around 120 knots the weight of the aircraft is carried by the forward canard wing and the lifting tail. This avoids the plumbing complexity of the X-wing since the rotor does not have to support the weight of the aircraft during transition. At this point the rotor can be stopped and stowed athwartships where it will function as a conventional wing, again using circulation control. The aircraft can now fly at high speed using jet thrust from the same powerplant that had been providing jet drive to the rotor during rotor-borne flight. The resulting flight envelope is, in many ways, like that of the V-22.

Fig 10.3 Boeing Canard Rotor/Wing *(Boeing)*

Helicopter Signatures

Under current British Army and US Doctrine, the helicopter plays a significant part in the deep battle. Heliborne assault and attack helicopter raids deep behind enemy lines are both seen as key operations in Manoeuvre Warfare. Key targets like command and control centres and ground-based air defence radar sites will be high priorities for AH raids, as will heavy concentrations of equipment and men in the enemy rear and close areas. Until now, helicopters could achieve a high degree of surprise, but with the advent of the airborne stand-off radar and ground- and air-based ESM systems, the balance will change. These radars, deployed in safe, protected airspace often many miles from the front line, will be largely immune to attack. Stationed within a fighter screen, they will be able to maintain a high-resolution active picture of the battlespace. Hostile attack or utility helicopters engaged in deep operations will be visible to the radar eye in the sky. Paradoxically, as ground-based radars become ever more vulnerable to SEAD and therefore less useful, the airborne radar, because of its relative invulnerability to attack, may well become the principal active surveillance sensor in the battlespace. Use of active systems like Longbow in terrain-mapping or terrain-following modes will bring with it a high probability of interception and therefore loss of surprise.

Radar Signatures

As a result of the risk from airborne radars, radar signature reduction and radar signature management will become key design drivers for new military helicopters. (Indeed, this will also be true of fixed wing aircraft, whose stealth features, if they have any, are optimised against ground-based systems looking up at them, rather than airborne radars looking down). Standard signature reduction methods, the use of radar absorbing materials and the shaping of structures to minimise reflectors, will continue to be important features of aircraft design. In the future, however, Active Cancellation techniques will become more common. Using Active Cancellation incoming radar signals are stored in a digital RF chip and then re-transmitted at an appropriate power half a wavelength out of phase from the natural radar echo. Only low power is required of the re-transmitter because traditional radar signature reduction techniques will have reduced the overall vehicle signature and concentrated it in known and predictable directions, which means that the active cancellation system only has to work on those axes. This technique may be of particular importance for the reduction of the rotor blade signature.

Acoustic Signatures

Helicopters have a very distinctive acoustic signature that can be exploited at considerable range. The main sources of helicopter noise are the main and tail rotors, although the gearbox and turbomachinery can also make significant contributions. Unlike jet noise, the directional characteristics of rotor noise are such that there is a strong forward propagation: an approaching helicopter can often be heard for up to five minutes.

There are three main types of rotor noise source: fluctuating rotor blade forces; so-called "thickness" noise due to the periodic displacement of air by the moving rotor; and "fluid stresses" due to viscosity in the air. These last two sources can become significant for very high-speed rotors but the first is generally considered most important for low-speed helicopters. There are several factors that contribute to fluctuating blade forces, from the cyclic lift changes needed for normal flight to turbulence and vortex shedding. One particular source is Blade Vortex Interaction (BVI), caused by the blade tip passing through the tip vortex shed by the preceding blade. This tends to occur during certain flight manoeuvres and gives rise to a characteristic "blade slap" noise. It can be particularly prominent on two-bladed rotors where each tip vortex is strong, or on multi-rotor helicopters. The Westland BERP tip might be expected to produce more BVI noise because of its strong vortex structure. Overall, however, it is significantly quieter than conventional rotor blades, especially at high speeds.

Tail rotors can be particularly noticeable sources of overall helicopter noise due to their high rotational speeds. They often have to operate in the wake of the main rotor and engine cowling, leading to interactions with turbulence and vortices. It is generally recognised now that these interactions are less severe if the tail rotor rotates so that it is moving aft at the top. Westland's Lynx Mk.7 introduced such a tail rotor and, by comparison with the Lynx Mk.1 which had the tail rotor moving forward at the top, reduced the noise by 10dB in some conditions. Further reductions in tail rotor noise can be obtained by shrouding, as in the fenestron design. This is reasonably effective in the forward direction and at high speed but the higher loading of the small ducted rotor leads to higher sideline noise. Perhaps the better alternative is the NOTAR design where the fan for the air-jet system is buried inside the base of the tail boom. Initially, this was a noisy system, with its small fan and high-speed jets but detailed development work, including putting the fan inlet on the top of the airframe and reducing the tip speed of the fan, has produced one of the quietest designs in the world. The NOTAR has been shown to be up to 7dB quieter in high-speed level flight than an equivalent MD 500E helicopter with open tail rotor.

Helicopter acoustic signatures (i.e. the variation of noise amplitude with frequency) are highly distinctive, being determined by the number of blades on the main and tail rotors and the rotational speeds of these two. Even at long ranges it is quite possible not only to classify the helicopter by type but also, by wavelet analysis, to determine the speed of the helicopter and its distance from the receiving sensor. Just as with modern artillery locating systems, a line of sensors will provide accurate positional data and even an accurate fire control solution. Research into the reduction of rotor noise is taking place in the US, UK and elsewhere and a number of improvements are being made. In general, helicopter noise goes up as the forward speed is increased but modern developments, such as the BERP tip are successfully countering this trend. Noise also increases markedly if the rotor blade tip speed is too high, so designs which can operate efficiently at reduced tip speeds are favourable. Acoustic signature is an area where there are very strong civil as well as military design drivers, so research effort is likely to continue and will produce further noise reductions.

Passive Millimetric Wave Imaging

At the moment, in 1999, passive millimetric wave imaging is very much an infant technology. Real time imaging has only become possible very recently and the sensors, generally the creation of government funded research centres, are bulky and expensive. Nevertheless, the technology is maturing fast and it will soon be possible to mount a passive surveillance sensor that can see through everything but the hardest rain. There are windows in the millimetric part of the electromagnetic spectrum at 35, 94, 140 and 220 GHz, but at the moment it is the two lower windows that offer the most benefit. Basically, metal objects, even painted ones, reflect the cold sky, presenting the receiver with a high-resolution passive picture. Until helicopters are constructed using non-reflective materials, or materials which mimic the emissivity of the natural background, the passive millimetric wave imager poses a significant threat. If, however, the next generation of helicopters were designed with a deliberately low signature in the millimetric range, an entire surveillance window would be closed before it had really opened.

Thermal Signature

Thermal signature is an area that is well understood in the helicopter community and, as a result, thermal signatures on modern helicopters are a fraction of what they were. Early IR homing missile systems, operating in the 3- 5-micron band and homing on the Doppler shifted CO_2 gas in the exhaust of a jet engine forced designers and manufacturers to minimise emissions. More recent seekers, however, have been designed to operate in the 8–14 micron band, where they are not looking for the intense signature generated by the exhaust, but are imaging the helicopter itself. The image generated by the seeker eye can be compared with a library of images that will give the missile a high degree of discrimination and false target rejection. The advent of these imaging seekers presents a formidable challenge for helicopter designers, not least because these imagers require only minimal thermal (in the order of 1 degree K) contrast in order to operate. It may well be that only active countermeasures, either 'soft' or 'hard' kill such as Nemesis or DIRCM/ATIRCM, will be the solutions to this very specific threat.

24-hour Capability

A surprising number of helicopters are advertised as being 'all weather' capable. Without exception, this is untrue. The current reliance on thermal imaging to provide the aircrew with a view of the world in darkness or thick haze means that those systems cannot operate in fog. Systems like Longbow radar can provide a reasonably high resolution picture with functions like terrain mapping, but they are active systems and therefore vulnerable to interception and jamming, and risk losing the element of surprise for the helicopter.

It is possible that no one sensor will be able to provide the helicopter with a true all weather capability. Instead, the information generated from a number of sensors and instruments will have to be fused together in order to present the pilot with an accurate representation of the world.

Positional Information

Currently GPS is the most popular modern navigational system fitted in today's military helicopters. It is accurate and reliable but according to recent reports, easily jammable by low powered transmitters that can be delivered by a great variety of means, including artillery. The current trend would appear to be towards almost total reliance on GPS for accurate positional data – a rather dangerous trend if the system is so easily degraded by local jamming. In order to guarantee navigational accuracy, inertial navigation, coupled to terrain matching by image comparison with 3D digital maps, would appear to be the only way of generating invulnerable positional data with sufficient accuracy to fly and fight safely in nil visibility.

Moving Maps

Accurate and timely digital mapping, with the raw data being gathered in near real time by satellite and downloaded either directly or indirectly to the aircraft may well form the core of the next generation of fully integrated flight control systems. With the advent of the 3 dimensional moving map, the aircraft sensors will be able to match the scene within its field of view with the map image. This will allow for aggressive flight in the nap of the earth and 'carefree handling' allowing the crew to concentrate on fighting the aircraft.

Optical and Passive Millimetric Wave Sensors

There are two types of active sensors currently being developed – the Honeywell Forward Looking Millimetric wave radar altimeter and the German laser based Hellas system. Both suffer from the same fundamental military flaw that they are active systems and therefore susceptible to interception by hostile ESM systems, despite the high attenuation through atmospheric absorption of the transmitted signal, particularly for the millimetric radar. Almost certainly this flaw will encourage the military to continue to concentrate development effort in passive systems, initially in thermal imaging, though fog will remain an impenetrable barrier, but increasingly in passive millimetric wave imaging. Real time imaging at

35Ghz is now possible and a prototype system suitable for a helicopter has been developed in the UK. Passive imaging at 94 GHz, the next window in that part of the spectrum, will allow large objects such as terrain features to be detected at long range in fog and small targets like power cables to be detected at short range. For example, a system capable of producing a high resolution image of wires 1000 feet ahead of a helicopter flying at 45 knots, will give the aircrew about 30 seconds warning, more than adequate time to take avoiding action.

Terrain-following Flight Control Systems and Sensor Data Fusion

A highly integrated navigation and collision avoidance system could be developed, based on 3D digital mapping with highly accurate inertial navigation and an imaging system that can terrain-match. From this it is only a small step to integrate those systems into a terrain-following flight control system that will effectively fly the aircraft, allowing the aircrew to fight the helicopter.

The Future Helicopter

Having identified some of the key technology drivers, it is worth speculating on what a future military helicopter might look like. For land warfare, one can see a requirement for at least two distinct types: the utility helicopter and the attack helicopter. For the purposes of this chapter it is assumed that both aircraft types will be crewed by aircrew, though it is clear that the human has become a largely redundant component in flying the machine. As long as civil transport aircraft are flown by humans, so will military utility helicopters. Whether or not the next generation of attack aircraft will be inhabited or not is hard to judge. The uninhabited solution is certainly tempting. The aircraft could be smaller and lighter and the flight control system less complex. The aircraft would be far more agile, as the human would no longer be the limiting factor in the extreme manoeuvre end of the flight envelope. Other fully autonomous vehicles, such as Global Hawk, will soon be able to conduct very long-range attack missions and there is a powerful and growing lobby, particularly in the USA, that advocates that all combat aircraft should be unmanned. This author cannot help but feel that the human component of any attack system is the critical component. In a nutshell, warfare is a human activity that requires blood to be spilt. Robotic warfare, conducted by machines operating autonomously, is not warfare.

The Future Utility Helicopter

The key design driver for the future utility helicopter will be its ability to transport a useful number of men and their equipment at high speed over long distances. Conventional helicopters have neither the speed nor the range and so the only obvious candidate is a convertiplane like the V-22. In transit it will be vulnerable to detection by airborne radars and so radar signature reduction through shaping and material will be a high priority. Having crossed the coast the aircraft will need to be able to fly fast in the nap of the earth, where it will be shielded from most ground-based sensors. An accurate navigational system coupled to an imaging sensor and an integrated terrain following/collision avoidance flight control system will allow the aircrew to fly aggressively in nil visibility close to the surface. A quietened rotor system will reduce the chance of interception by hostile acoustic sensors and the aircraft will have a low thermal signature.

It may well be, though, that there is a requirement for a second type of helicopter to augment the tiltrotorcraft. The US Marine Corps and the US Navy have both conducted trials of the Kaman K-Max helicopter in the support role and it is possible that the helicopter could be used as a specialist loadlifter and may even be unmanned. It would seem to have the great advantages of cheapness, low running costs and the capability to lift 2722 kg externally and it will be interesting to watch if other armed services take an interest in this novel machine.

Fig 10.4 K-Max *(Kaman Aerospace)*

The Future Attack Helicopter

Speed, agility, a low signature and the ability to detect and identify targets at long range will be key drivers for the future attack helicopter. The aircraft will be small and almost certainly single seat. A highly capable flight control system will allow real carefree handling, with the aircraft capable of being flown fully hands-off in nil visibility in the nap of the earth. The crewman will be able to concentrate his efforts in fighting the command and weapons system. The principal target acquisition sensor will be a passive millimetric wave imager, which will be used to localise and identify the targets. Raw target information will have been datalinked to the aircraft by the airborne stand-off sensor aircraft, similar to ASTOR and AWACS but fitted with both active and passive synthetic aperture sensors. In due course, the attack helicopter will become uninhabited and will operate with a high degree of autonomy under the overall control of the airborne sensor.

Fig 10.5 Artists impression of a naval CR/W *(Boeing)*

Possibly, the aircraft will be of CRW type, flying like a helicopter at lower speeds and like a fixed wing at high speeds. The aircraft will be optimised for a low radar signature against airborne stand-off systems and will not reflect at millimetric frequencies.

The Future Maritime Helicopter

Unlike its land counterparts, the ship-based helicopter is much more likely to be a jack of all trades rather than a master of one. It must be capable of transferring stores and personnel, carrying out search and rescue missions and conducting a wide range of combat missions using a range of weapons and sensors. As a result of these widely disparate demands, the design of such an aircraft will always be a compromise. In addition, stowage and operating space will always be at a premium, requiring the aircraft to have expensive and weighty blade folding gear and robust undercarriages. It will have to be designed to operate in the maritime environment – a wet, salt-laden atmosphere that will drive the designer towards the large-scale use of non-metallic composite materials and light non-magnesium based alloys. In addition, naval aircraft must be fully electro-magnetically compatible with the ships from and with which they operate.

All the above leads one to speculate that the future maritime helicopter will be a scaled-down version of the V-22. It will have a good load lifting capability and room for a number of passengers. Capable of being fitted with a wide range of weapons and sensors and built largely of composites, but foldable so that it can fit into the hangar of a medium-sized warship.

Summary

Some future trends in military helicopter design have been identified, based on currently perceived military requirements and on recent research. Higher speeds, reduced signatures and increased operability have been identified as over-riding themes. Of these higher transit speed, reduced acoustic signatures (and lower vibration levels) and some aspects of increased operability will also be of interest to the civil community; this could increase the chances of some of these predictions coming to fruition. As for fixed-wing aircraft, it is likely that radar stealth will prove too expensive for many designers and operators so it is unlikely that there will be many "stealth" helicopters in the future.

Index